MW00773389

"In '99% A Human, 1% Amazing,' Daryl Williams Jr. explored how the journey of a teacher transcends the boundaries of the classroom. He offers a profound narrative that resonates with every educator's heart. This is not just a book; it's a beacon of hope and a testament to the extraordinary potential within each and every educator! Daryl masterfully intertwines personal struggle with professional triumph, revealing the superhero within every teacher. This compelling book serves as a reminder that within the challenges of teaching lies the power to inspire, innovate, and transform lives. A must-read for anyone in the noble pursuit of shaping future generations."

—**Shaun Woodly, Ph.D.**, CEO & Founder, Teach Hustle Inspire

"A perfect balance between daily motivation phrases and actionable ways to support teens at home and school through their journey to self-discovery."

—**Shekeria Barnes**, Founding Principal, Southwest Charlotte STEM Academy

"This book is an easy-to-follow guide to help teachers and students find their way. Daryl uses his own personal experience to help others understand the power of recognizing and operating in your differences."

—**Michelle Pierce**, 2021 Amazon Future Engineer Teacher of the Year

"It left me on the edge of my seat so many times. Tremendously written. It is so real, and so much of what we go through as educators on a daily basis. This was a masterpiece."

—**Clay Sanders**, District Athletic Director

Acknowledgements

"You aren't as strong as your dream; you are as strong as your team."

— 99% A Human, 1% Amazing | Page 144

I am extremely grateful for the team that helped to make this dream come true.

Andrea Person
Ashley Hill
Brandon J. Watkins
Carla Forbes
Charles McGill
Clay Sanders
Dr. Shaun Woodly
Imogen Thomas-Williams
Jamal Tate
Jazzi Goode
Manley Moore
Megan Pierce
Michelle Pierce
Morel Williams
Rodney Johnson
Sandra Caldwell
Shekeria Barnes
Teddy McIlwain Jr.
Travon Wallace

99%
A》》HUMAN,
1% AMAZING

EMPOWERING EDUCATORS TO
OVERCOME STRESS, AVOID BURNOUT,
AND CREATE IMPACTFUL CHANGE

DARYL WILLIAMS JR.

ISBN: 979-8-9894878-0-6

Classroom Management Book, Teaching Strategies Book, Teacher Self-Improvement, Classroom Management Ideas, Classroom Management for Teachers, Teacher Resources, Educational Leadership Books

Contents

To my children, Nyelle and Joel: Daddy loves you. I always have, I always will, no matter what. You are amazing. Don't settle for *good* because you're destined for *great*. Love yourself so much that there is no room for hate. Know that you were made by a God that makes no mistakes.

To my wife, Shakira: You are such a blessing. Out of everything that's happened to me...you're the best thing.

Introduction

"I just want to teach."

– Teachers Everywhere

This is not a story I share often because it is as embarrassing as it is painful. In the Spring of 2015, during the second semester of my first-year teaching, I hit the figurative and literal lowest point in my career. I laid in the fetal position on the floor in the middle of the hallway asking myself, "Why am I doing this?"

You may be wondering how I ended up there. Trust me, it was not the plan. The day started like any other day. Birds were singing, the wind was blowing, my homeroom was terrorizing me; nothing out of the ordinary. During my 2nd period planning when I was expected to reorganize my classroom, grade exit tickets, plan the following weeks lessons, make copies, cover a class, follow-up on student discipline, meet with my team, conference with parents, respond to emails, eat my lunch, and have a moment to breathe, I decided to go make copies. As I was walking to the copy room, I noticed two eighth grade boys who I did not teach posturing as if they were about to fight. We were the only three in the hallway at the time, and I figured that as the adult, I had to something. So, I sprang into action. Spoiler alert: I made the wrong choice.

I shouted, "Hey! Get to class!"

They heard me, but decided to ignore that command, and go with option B instead; beat on each other relentlessly. Now that things had gotten physical, I figured that as the adult, I had to do something else. I made yet another bad decision.

I ran up to the dueling duo and inserted myself in between them in an effort to break it up. "Surely since an adult has intervened, they will stop."- I thought to myself. They did not. As a matter of fact, I believe it gave them an increased level of commitment to finish what they started. Punches kept flying around and into me. Then, to make matters worse, the two decided to bear hug each other and take this party to the ground. Since I was sandwiched in between them, I had to go along for the ride.

We hit the floor in one quick motion, with my left knee meeting the tile first. At this point, lying on the floor in the fetal position between them as they continued to fight, I finally made a good decision. I opened my mouth and yelled, "Yo!" as if to say, "Somebody, anybody, come do something about this!" My cry for help had the same effect as the bat symbol, alerting the gym teacher, Coach Wells, that I was in distress. He came down the hall and broke up the fight. He helped me up and asked me if I was ok. With a sharp throbbing pain in my knee, panting breath, half-undone bowtie, and my heart racing, I gave him the obvious response.

"I'm fine," I said, in an effort to appear as if that charade went exactly as planned. He took the boys to the office, and I limped back to my room with the crumpled paper that I intended to copy.

Back in my room, I sat at my desk. I looked at the overturned chairs, scraps of paper all over the desks, smushed raisins on the floor from breakfast, names and checks on the board from my faulty management system, and the data wall that looked like the Spanish flag with its combination of red and yellow. I just stared for a moment. After some time passed, I said audibly in my empty classroom, "I just want to teach."

Although this situation was an anomaly, it was very on-brand for my first-year teaching. I struggled daily from August until June. I, like many teachers, had a very different expectation of what teaching would be like. I thought I would be able to manage the classroom. After all, during the two weeks that we spent learning classroom management in college, I was a pro! The fact that I graduated High School led me to believe that I could easily teach 7th graders math. My end-of-year average student growth score of -2.6 ended that belief. I fully expected parents to partner with me and hold their children accountable for their actions. Heated debates with parents enabling their child's misbehavior proved that to be a fantasy. That year was the hardest year of my life. I was a terrible teacher. I was such a terrible teacher that it wasn't a secret. During a conversation years later, an administrator from my first year told me that they discussed letting me go after year one. The only saving grace for me was that math teachers are hard to find.

Being completely honest, I was ready to quit. I saw what they saw and figured that I was doing a disservice to students and that I wasn't cut out for this work. I felt as if what was being asked of me was more than I was capable of doing. I felt as if my hard work was being disrespected, and my caring heart was being abused. I felt as if students would be better off with someone else, and I know I am not the only one who has ever felt this way.

If you are a teacher who is certain that you want to return to teaching next school year, you are the minority. According to a 2022 survey by The National Education Association, 55% of teachers admit they are thinking of leaving the profession. This is especially true in a post-pandemic era where students are so far behind, it could take as much as a decade before we see students in class who haven't been impacted by it.

Teachers are tired. Buried under mountains of paperwork, laboring under the weight of district, state, and federal regulation, and facing the new era of students who don't always bring a natural love and desire for school, are enough to make any teacher rethink their profession. Old methods are ineffective, most curriculum is outdated, and many resources are lacking. Not to mention, teacher pay has failed to keep pace with that of other professions who have seen their yearly salaries rise consistently. Goals are being set in the wrong way or so unrealistically, they are impossible to achieve. Yet, in the midst of these challenges, teachers are expected to produce students who still perform well on standardized tests. If you connect with any of the above just nod silently to yourself; nobody will notice.

I felt all these things and had one foot out the door, but I learned something that saved my career, and I hope it resonates with you as well.

Right at the end of that first year, before I decided whether I was going to return or not, a statement in a commencement speech changed my whole life. I was at my wife Shakira's graduation, and the commencement speaker must have known what I was struggling with. I bet most of the people there tuned him out, anxious for the ceremony to end. For some reason, I was dialed in. I suppose that, subconsciously, I was anxious for answers. The words he spoke penetrated my being when he said:

Never underestimate your impact!

He went on to explain that somebody needs what we have to offer. They may not know how to ask for it, they may not always show appreciation for it, but they will be better because of it. He talked about how we can't let the uncomfortable feeling of inadequacy stop us from figuring out how to make our impact. I thought about my "why," or the reason I became an educator. I thought about the students that deserved to have teachers that care about them as much as I do. I thought about the massive impact I could have if I was able to become a highly effective educator. In that very moment I decided that I was going to figure it out; and that is what I did.

That summer, I took the opportunity to do more research than I had ever done before. I studied how to become a better leader and what teaching methods were most effective in reaching today's students. I didn't restrict my studies to the field of education. I looked at the work of successful people across many industries and what they learned about successful leadership. What I uncovered was not what I expected, but exactly what I needed to find. I learned that there was not a perfect recipe for success. Many have demonstrated effective leadership, but not everyone's path was the same. Each person was able to achieve success by matching proven principles with their own unique gifts and talents. This helped me to understand that to make the impact I dreamed of, I had to leverage my uniqueness.

The reason my students weren't growing during my first year was because while I was trying to implement research-based practices, I failed to incorporate my unique gifts and talents. I tried so hard to model after others that I forgot to highlight what set me apart. I tried to impact through the 99% of me that was just like everyone else, when I should've prioritized the 1% that makes me amazing. We'll dive deeper into that statement in Chapter 5.

I knew what I had to do. I needed to find out what made me unique, and allow my differences to make a difference. That is exactly what I did, and it worked.

I clearly identified my dream outcomes for students, harnessed my unique abilities, fortified my mindset against doubt, and transformed unmotivated students to empowered achievers. The result, I transitioned from being a terrible teacher to a two-time "Teacher of the Year."

I always say that becoming a "Teacher of the Year" was never the goal. It was just a by-product of me understanding **The Four ID's** of my teacher identity. I became a transformative teacher by understanding how to do the following:

Identify My **D**ream
Illuminate My **D**ifferences
Ignore My **D**oubters
Improve My **D**ata

My goal now is to help as many teachers as possible go further faster. The information in this book is a detailed blueprint of how I was able to make the transition described earlier. I will tell you about the lessons I've learned, the strategies that I have seen work consistently, and things I wish I knew while I was going through the struggle. In true teacher fashion, be prepared to annotate, respond, and reflect as we go through the chapters. Get ready to be vulnerable as we do thought-provoking exercises that uncover what *your* "1% Amazing" is. After all, my goal is not to make you the next best version of me or anyone else, but to help you become the very best version of yourself. You can only do that by learning how to leverage your uniqueness, and I will show you how.

Before we begin, though, let me address what might be a nagging question in your mind: "How am I going to be uniquely me and use ground-breaking methods in a school where the administration is unsupportive, and the atmosphere in the building is not conducive for innovation?" It's a great question. So often, teachers are blocked from making changes the administration hasn't approved and teachers get all kinds of pushback. Even their fellow teachers can resent a teacher's success when they themselves are struggling.

Have no fear. In Chapter 10 I will show you how to get buy-in from the administration in ways that will not only support your efforts, but that will help to transform the culture of your school building. I will also show you how to collaborate with other teachers, and with the students, in an effective way that makes them your allies rather than your detractors.

I've spent years developing this system. Now I want to share that research and experience with you. What can you expect? You will gain clarity of your purpose and increase efficacy in your practice. You will reignite your love of teaching as your students will develop a love of learning. You will see both measurable and immeasurable results in your students. You will be able to revive your dream of a long and prosperous teaching career. I can tell you that it won't be easy, but I can also tell you that it's worth it. You can do hard things. You've got this, and I've got you. Let's get started.

For free bonuses and digital versions of the exercises in this book, scan the code below or visit:

www.onepercentamazing.com/resources

SECTION **1**

Identify Your Dream

Chapter 1 – What Do You Want?

"Teaching is the greatest act of optimism." – Colleen Wilcox

When you started teaching, what was the driving motivation behind that decision? Why not be a plumber, an accountant, or a ballet dancer? You rejected the millions of different career paths available to you and chose teaching. There must have been a compelling reason. I think it was because you know two things. First, there is nothing more amazing than a job that changes lives. Only a small segment of jobs can claim that they have a direct impact on a person's future. Additionally, you believe that you have the ability to make a massive impact.

As the founder of the Pursuit of Excellence, it is my mission to help a million students live the life that they choose, not the life that they settle for. In order to further the mission, I empower teachers by giving tips, tools, and resources to maximize student growth. Helping students realize their full potential is what I have always wanted and, I believe, is what most teachers want.

So, what happens? What gets teachers off track, feeling frustrated, considering other options, and recognizing that they aren't get paid enough for the grief they have to endure?

I think that with all the talk about creating environments that are ripe for learning, we forget about creating environments that are conducive for teaching. Inadequate classrooms, lack of technology, and ineffective training, are some of the many hurdles today's teachers have to face. But the place where teachers are most sorely lacking — even those with state-of-the-art physical environments — is the support, appreciation, and encouragement teachers need.

You are enough!

This is the primary message of this book. You will receive lots of tips on how to elevate your work to produce stellar learners. That in no way suggests that right now, who you are, you are inadequate. If you are not yet producing the outcomes that you envisioned, you can acquire the skills that will allow you to do so. The gap between where you are and where you want to be, is the acquisition of skills that you don't yet have. Understand that you are smart enough to acquire those skills. If it is possible, you are capable.

You are enough. That's right. Who you are right now is enough to change a child's life forever in a positive way. This is something that not enough teachers understand. We celebrate teacher appreciation week once a year and think that is sufficient for teachers to understand that they wield incredible power. There are teachers right now in run-down schools, where students share old and battered books, and there is little to no technology. Even that teacher, in the worst of situations, has a special magic that can change a child's life.

We tend to want to be copycats and mimic some other teacher. I know this was the case for me. I watched the Ron Clark movie and immediately tried to learn how to Double Dutch, and dance. I made a class incentive that if they earned enough points I would have to dance in front of the class. It went so poorly that it had the opposite effect of what it was supposed to. Students didn't even laugh at me, which would have been a fun relationship building moment. They just stared and didn't comment. Afterwards, a student came up to me and asked if next time they could just have free time as their reward. They would rather sit and do nothing than sit and watch me struggle through the Nae Nae again.

Sometimes it is good to learn from those who are having success and what is working effectively in somebody else's classroom. But we often forget that it's not the bells and whistles that make a teacher amazing. We forget our special touch and, instead of trying to *imitate* good teachers, we try to *replicate* them. Instead of modeling after their practices and making them our own, we want to be exactly like them and do the exact thing they do.

The most effective thing teachers can do is be the best version of themselves rather than a knockoff version of somebody else.

I'll repeat, you are enough! You always have been, and you always will be.

Two things

There are two things that need to happen for you to know and believe that you are enough. Being grounded and committed — this is the golden combination for ultimate success. You will feel effective and feed your mind, spirit, and soul. You will know that you are enough.

1. Be Grounded

Perhaps you marvel, as I often do, that even in the greatest storms, ones strong enough to slide cars across the highway and pull roofs off houses, trees manage to remain. The reason is because they are grounded by a strong root system. While most trees survive the storm, a handful are lifted up and tossed around. When you check their roots systems, it becomes clear why. They were not grounded. Their roots were shallow, diseased, pest-ridden, or suffering some other malady that made the trees vulnerable to the winds and the rains of the storm.

It's time to be grounded. The path to get there is to first understand that you are an **expert**. Often as teachers, we assume that we are not good enough in our own right. We believe that we don't have what it takes to truly be an educator. In reality, you are an **expert in your own experience.** Whether you are a first-year teacher or a veteran with a decade under his or her belt, you are an expert in your own experience.

The unique experiences that you have had in your life have shaped the unique perspectives you carry with you as you go throughout your duties every single day. No, you are not the only teacher in your building, but you are the only *you*. Only you can do what you do as nobody else has had the experiences you have had.

Millions of people used telephones every day, but there was something in Steve Jobs' experience that caused him to view the telephone with a different perspective. The iPhone came from his unique take on the world. He had the same access to telephones as others, but he had a different expertise. His uniqueness allowed him to create devices that connect people all over the world from something small enough to fit in our pockets! He was able to do that because of his experience and how it shaped the lens through which he saw the world.

That and millions of other examples serve as the basis for my belief that, while there are millions of teachers, there is no one in the world who can do what you do.

What does it mean to be grounded?

When a teacher loves his or her work, it's tough to see several students in a class fail a test or struggle to grasp a concept without wondering how to make it better. The best teachers take the failure of their students as a challenge to find a new way to impart the concept. You feel like you need to be something else or someone else. You assume that another teacher, a better teacher, would have been more successful. As a result, you are not grounded.

As an instructional coach, I had a bout with what it feels like to lose my grounding. My role and responsibilities were curriculum, instruction, and assessment. I made curricular decisions and used the data from assessments to inform instruction and coach teachers on how to improve.

One day, I was going through a stack of data, trying to understand what was happening in a particular classroom. I needed to make sense of the numbers I was seeing so I could coach a teacher appropriately. Just then, someone popped in my office and said the most unusual thing: "Wow, it must be nice to be able to sit in your office all day." I felt the pain of that statement because, in that person's eyes, I wasn't working hard. I altered my practice to do more of the analysis at night or early in the day so that I could spend my days walking around the school. I became more visible in the hallways, fist bumping students, encouraging staff, providing bathroom breaks, and visiting classrooms to offer support. One day as I was making my rounds, I stepped into a teacher's classroom to offer support, and she said to me, "Wow, it must be nice to just walk around smiling all day."

At that moment, I realized that you can't teach or work for other's approval. I went back to my office and decided that I needed to get grounded in what I was called to do, so that I was not operating based off others' perspectives but based on my purpose.

I had to come to terms with the fact that I actually like sitting at my desk, dissecting data and performing root cause analysis. I love meeting with teachers, discussing their concerns and figuring out the right solutions. I love interacting with students and helping them understand that they can learn anything. I love to coach teachers and have those one-on-one conversations as we dig into the data and I explain what I'm seeing. I am overjoyed when they use my tips to be more engaging and help their students. That's who I am and what I do!

So, I sat down at my desk, and asked myself how I could ground myself in operating in my Zone of Excellence. Here is what I came up with:

My Dream

Think of it as a triangle where the foundation is your dream, or "What you WANT to do." This is the force that drives you. What is it that you wake up in the morning with a passion for? How do you envision yourself leaving an impact on this world? What is it that you *want* to do when you step foot in that building?

My Duties

One of the walls of the triangle is your duties, or "What you HAVE to do." This is what you are contractually obligated to do per your employer. We all have specific duties that we have to attend to on a daily basis that cannot be ignored. What did you sign up and agree to do? What do school and district leaders expect you to be doing on a consistent basis? What is it that you *have* to do, when you are on work hours?

My Desires

The other wall of the triangle is your desires, or "What you LIKE to do." This is what you enjoy about your current position. What are those perks that come with the job? What are some of the unique allowances that your role provides? It is common for the shortfalls to be highlighted, but let's not ignore the positives. There are many enjoyable things about what you decided to do. What is it that you *like* to do when you are on the job?

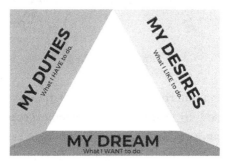

My Reality

The triangle has been formed. I spent time thinking about myself and listed my dream, my duties, and my desires. I thought about my role and listed what I want to do, what I have to do, and what I like to do. After I wrote these things down, I decided to synthesize them into one single statement. I put that statement inside the triangle and realized that what I uncovered by listing what I want to do, what I have to do, and what I like to do, was what I GET to do. I *get* to do these things on a consistent basis. I *get* to show up this way in my school building. I *get* to have an impact that no one else can have. That is my reality.

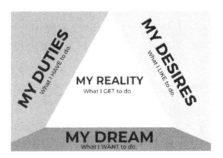

When you pull these pieces into alignment, you will get to show up each day fulfilled, grounded, and understanding that you are enough. You will feel driven and inspired. No longer will you worry so much about what others are doing or their opinions about your methods.

This is important because even though you're not the only fourth grade teacher, or music teacher, or team lead in your building, you will find that everyone's answers are different. Even amongst those with similar roles, your reality is unique to you. You are special, and that's why you are needed.

Now it is your turn. Take a few moments to reflect below, to determine what you GET to do, so that you can be grounded in your role.

For free bonuses and a digital version of this exercise, scan the code below or visit:

www.onepercentamazing.com/resources

Reflection Worksheet

What do you <u>want</u> to do?

What is your dream? What do you want to do as a teacher?

What do you <u>have</u> to do?

What are your duties?

What do you <u>like</u> to do?

What are your desires?

What do you <u>get</u> to do?

How can you condense your responses to just one statement that describes your reality?

2. Be Committed.

Being committed is hard. Let's just admit that. It's especially difficult at the end of the school year as you are thinking about your future. You think back to the start of the school year when you needed support and there was little help available. Why are the same teachers who were supposed to be collaborating with you talking about you behind your back? How can you be committed to this work for years and years with all the challenges you face?

You remember, at the lowest point in my career, I was literally on the floor calling for help, sandwiched between two eighth grade boys who were fighting. I returned to my classroom in pain and in shock over the incident. I sat in my chair thinking about everything I had experienced and asked that fateful question:

Why am I doing this?

I had spent tens of thousands of dollars on tuition and countless hours in study, practice, and work only to end up rolling on the floor with two boys who were attacking each other.

I was in despair. After all, I just wanted to be a good teacher. I just wanted to make a difference. I then grounded myself in my purpose and remained committed to making an impact.

We may never know how much we matter. If we're lucky, we might learn about it years later in a surprise Facebook message from an ex-student. But we only make a difference if we never underestimate the impact we are having on students.

I committed at that point to say that I would keep going and figure this thing out. I was grounded enough in my reason why and was finally able to see that I was making a difference even when it didn't seem as if I was.

Your success is not tied to your resources; it's about your resourcefulness! It's about your grit and tenacity. You may not have access to all the technologies or books or resources you think you need. But if you are grounded and keep your focus on what you get to do every single day, it can help you remain committed.

When you are grounded in the work that you are doing, commit to seeing it through, you will maximize your impact. I am not saying you should sacrifice your body and break up fights, I actually **strongly** advise against that. I am saying that there will always be things that bother you, but when you are committed, you won't let them beat you. Is it going to be hard? Definitely. But you are smarter than you think, you are braver than you feel, you are stronger than you seem, and you can do hard things. Commit to doing what you *get* to do.

Chapter 2: Where Are You Going?

"Education is not the filling of a pail but the lighting of a fire."

– William Butler Yeats

What's the vision you have for your classroom?

It's a gigantic question, I know. It has answers that are educational, social, emotional, logistical, and more. But so many teachers have answered this question in the past only to see the school year unfold in a way they didn't want or plan.

We explored the statistic earlier that 55% of teachers are considering not coming back to the classroom. The reason why so many teachers are not returning is not just because the school year is difficult or challenging. It is because the vision they had seems to be moving farther and farther away. They simply don't see things getting any better.

There is an old, very popular adage that says, "Without a vision, the people perish." Many teachers are perishing, walking around like zombies having lost the heart for teaching. Once a teacher's heart is not in it, his or her mind won't be in it either because they don't see a vision of things getting any better. That is why so many give up and move on to corporate America or running their own business. They want to see their visions realized.

What do we have to do to ensure that every teacher has the best school year? It starts with identifying what that looks like and then envisioning ourselves living it.

People don't leave where they are until they see where they'd rather be.

As teachers, it's critical to cast a vision for what we want in our classrooms, specifying what we want the school year to look like. Emmy Award winning comedian and show host, Steve Harvey, will tell you that he attributes all of his success to vision casting and making it visible by placing it on a vision board. He stated that everything he's gotten in life was written down first on a goal sheet and posted on a vision board.

Many successful celebrities and CEOs report the same success. For example, of the 50 issues of O Magazine, Oprah Winfrey is on the cover of nearly every one. It was a running joke that no one else would be allowed to grace the cover. But Emmy Award winning comedian, Ellen DeGeneres, created a vision board showing herself on the cover. And sure enough, she was one of the handful of people to be asked. Singer and rapper, Cardi B, talked about vision casting and having a fashion line that she wanted to be a hit long before her Fashion Nova collection sold out within hours of being launched. Best-selling author Jack Canfield placed his vision board, depicting himself as a best-selling author receiving a million dollar check above his bed so it was the first thing he saw when he woke each day.

It's all about having a vision, writing it down, and making it visible. The visibility of the vision makes it easier to chase and, ultimately, make it a reality. Robyn Jackson suggests that a vision is something that we want to be true for 100% of our students. Envision what you want to be true for 100% of your students this school year. Avoid setting goals like achieving 70% mastery, as that leaves out fully 30% of your students. Instead, focus on a vision that includes every single student in your class.

If you can see it, you can be it.

The brain works in a strange way. When it believes that something is true, it works to bring that reality to us. The brain never sleeps. It is always in motion — strategizing, synergizing, and searching out cues in our environment. If you believe that you've already seen the best in a situation, you probably have. If you think that the status quo is the best you're going to get, your vision caps at the place you are and things are not likely to get any better.

On the other hand, if you allow yourself to dream, imagine, step out of the box, and remove barriers, you can grow and envision the reality you want. You start to imagine what success looks, feels, sounds, and tastes like. Once you do that, you are not far from achieving it.

One easy way to do this is by thinking about what your school year is going to look like. Imagine it as the best school year you've ever had. Start by asking three questions that help you cast your vision.

For free bonuses and a digital version of this exercise, scan the code below or visit:

www.onepercentamazing.com/resources

1. Why am I an educator?

Most of us haven't done this in a long time. Perhaps your why is the same as always. But it's just as likely that your why has changed.

My initial why was connected to not having a black male educator until I was a senior in high school. He was teaching African American History… go figure. I became an educator because I wanted people who looked like me to see somebody who looked like me.

Over time, that changed. Nine years later, my why today is that I want to give students the option to live the life that they choose and not a life that they're forced to settle for. I want to help them create choices through life skills, mindsets, and character development so that once they leave school, they have the choice to follow their dreams.

2. What are your core values, principles, and beliefs?

If you can identify your core values, principles, and beliefs, they will drive everything that takes place in your classroom from curricular decisions to behavior management techniques. They will form the culture of your classroom. For example, if you believe in collaboration, anyone who enters your classroom will recognize that. It will be bright, active, noisy with an air of controlled chaos. Students will be communicating with one another in an atmosphere fired by the synergy and energy of collaboration.

That's going to look a lot different than somebody who believes in independent realization. That atmosphere might be more Zen with soft lighting. Students might be in their favorite spots with their laptops or devices.

When teachers are confident in their core values, principles, and beliefs, students will assimilate to the vibe of that classroom. But when there's a disconnect between what the teacher identifies as core values, principles, and beliefs and what the teacher actually does in the classroom, students kick back because of the confusion and discord in the teacher's mindset and actions.

What troubles you more than anything else?

Sometimes what troubles us can also serve as our inspiration. Personally, what bothers me more than anything else is when somebody's living a life that they were forced to settle for because they didn't have the choice to do something else. When they lack the skills, resources, knowledge, drive, or motivation they need, I feel a deep sense of regret for them. If a person wants to be at Waffle House, they will do an amazing job, much like the waitress who won the lottery and went back to waitressing because she loved it. But the waitress who wanted to be a nurse will always wonder what could have been. Whether there were financial constraints, lack of required grades, or challenges passing the NCLEX exam, it bothers me that she couldn't chase her dream. That is why I work so hard to help people create choices.

What about you? What are the things that trouble you to the core? Think about the aspects that truly bother you, as they can serve as a source of inspiration.

As you create your vision, consider how what is so special about you can address the things that trouble you the most. Then focus on specific skills to improve your teaching practice, ensuring that the next school year becomes your best one yet.

Chapter 3: Who Are You?

"If you look behind every exceptional person there is an exceptional teacher." — Stephen Hawking

There are four types of teachers, but only one leads to true transformation. Does this surprise you to hear? Let's explore those four types of teachers and how three of them stand in the way of student growth and mastery.

All teachers at one point or another think about the three elements that are required to prepare for a school year. We all need goals, we all need a game plan, and we all need grit to get the job done.

To implement meaningful changes in your classroom, you need to master these essential elements. Let's explore each one as we think about who we are as teachers.

Goals

Having clear and well-defined goals is the first crucial step towards the change you want to see. Goals provide direction and purpose to your efforts.

Game Plan

Alongside your goals, you must develop concrete plans to achieve them. These plans outline the specific steps and strategies you'll use to reach your objectives.

Grit

Grit is your passion, motivation, and determination to see the change through. It's the inner fire that keeps you going even in the face of challenges.

Once these elements are in place, they are expressed in the context of who you are as a teacher. There are different teacher archetypes that are defined based on their mastery of these elements. See if you can see yourself in any of these:

The Thinker

This teacher has goals and a game plan but lacks the drive to implement them effectively. They have plenty of ideas and may maintain elaborate journals and data trackers. However, they struggle to act and translate their ideas into results. They are high on potential, but low on progress.

The Talker

This teacher possesses goals and grit, but they lack a concrete plan to achieve their objectives. They are vocal about their aspirations and goals which often leads to student motivation. However, without a well-thought-out plan, their efforts may lead to limited success. Their students get lost in the teachers' barrage of words.

The Treadmill Teacher

This teacher is highly enthusiastic, has plans, and possesses grit, but they lack a clear overarching goal. They may see pockets of success here and there, but without a unifying vision, their efforts may not result in transformative change. They see progress, but don't reach their peak.

The Transformative Teacher

To achieve true transformation and become a transformative teacher, you must marry all three elements. A combination of clear goals, detailed game plans, and unwavering grit, can lead to meaningful change and allows you to be your authentic self in the classroom.

When you master these three elements, you can be goofy, cool, or even corny in your teaching style, and students will respect and engage with you because they see your dedication and commitment to your goals. Your personality, quirks, and pet peeves will not overshadow your effectiveness as a teacher and your ability to connect with your students.

Remember, having goals, a game plan, and grit will drive everything in your classroom. Their impact will affect everything from managing your classroom to building strong relationships with your students. Embracing these elements is the key to achieving true transformation in your teaching practice.

Chapter 4: Avoid Becoming Overwhelmed

"Rest and self-care are so important. When you take time to replenish your spirit, it allows you to serve from the overflow. You cannot serve from an empty vessel."

—Eleanor Brown

How can you chase the dream that you have for students without getting burned out? We have started each chapter with a question for reflection, but this might be the one I hear most often. Teachers want to help their students but need to protect their own hearts and mind from constant disappointment, difficulty, pushback, etc.

Sometimes students don't show the expected progress, especially in the face of district mandates and administrative suggestions. This can lead to disinterested students and over-engaged parents, creating a challenging situation for teachers. How do we avoid getting overwhelmed with so many people to please?

In this chapter we will cover a three-part framework to help you avoid feeling overwhelmed this school year.

I once encountered a situation that prompted me to learn how to play the bass guitar. I was doing it because I wanted to help my church's choir. They needed more musicians, and I took up the challenge. I knew that it was going to take practice, and I had made a commitment to perform. I refused to let them down and knew that I would grow into the person I needed to be to make it happen.

The night before I was to perform, I was practicing trying to be my best for the next day. Suddenly, the strings felt like they were on fire. I looked at my hands and saw that the skin on my fingers were tearing apart and breaking off because of the callouses that formed. I chuckled and said to myself, "Maybe I overdid it."

Just like I committed to playing the bass guitar for my church's choir, you have committed to being the teacher who helps students grow, no matter the challenges. Even if you don't feel fully ready at this moment, making the commitment means you believe in your ability to evolve and become the teacher your students need.

However, as you carry out your commitment, remember the importance of self-care. Just as I ended up with calloused fingers from excessive practice, pushing yourself too hard can lead to pain and burnout. It's crucial to set boundaries and take care of yourself, ensuring you are available and energized to show up for your students every day.

I was pushing myself too hard, neglecting my own well-being for the sake of my mission. However, that's not the right approach. While commitment is essential, we must prioritize self-care and not become overwhelmed. If you are so overwhelmed that you underperform, are you making the impact that you were called to have?

During the 2023-2024 NFL season, the New York Jets made this point very clear. The Jets were in the market for a difference-maker at the Quarterback position. They seemed to have promise at other positions, but for years they struggled at the most important position in football. They decided to make a franchise-altering move and acquired four-time MVP Aaron Rogers and gave him a $75 million contract. Rogers' signing immediately made the New York Jets favorites to win the NFL's most coveted prize; the Super Bowl.

During the offseason, the hype only continued to increase. Every major sports network labeled the New York Jets as a team to watch during the season. Players, coaches, and fans were all-in on the potential for tremendous success. That all changed on September 11, 2023.

In a packed stadium for a primetime game, four plays into the game, Aaron Rogers went down with a season ending injury to his Achilles. Suddenly, his four MVP awards didn't matter so much. His ability to make quick decisions on offense was not helpful as he stood on the sideline all season. His ability to throw deep down the field with precise accuracy could not help them when the game was on the line. This event made it clear that in sports, an athlete's best ability is not their ability to run fast, jump high, or throw far. Their best ability is their availability to show up when it is gametime. When their availability is prohibited, the rest of the abilities don't matter.

For teachers, your best ability is not your teaching method, or your ability to write in a straight line on the whiteboard. Your best ability is your availability to show up mentally and physically for students. None of your other abilities can show up if your availability is shut down. If you are stressed, overwhelmed, and burnt out, you are not available to be your best self.

To avoid burnout, set limits on working hours and take breaks for family and personal time. Don't let stress and work consume you; learn to control what you can and let go of the rest. Remember, it's okay not to be perfect; focus on doing your best in the present moment. Rather than trying to master everything at once, take baby steps, and work on improving each day. It's not about the speed of your progression, but that you are moving in the right direction.

Finally, focus on "chewing" the bite-sized chunks of your goals. You don't need to consume the whole buffet, just chew one bite at a time. Focus on what you can handle at each moment. Avoid overwhelming yourself by trying to tackle everything at once. Steady progress in the right direction is more important than rushing towards the finish line. Take baby steps, master each chunk, and strive to improve incrementally.

SECTION **2**

Illuminate Your Differences

Chapter 5: Your Unique Abilities

"Teaching kids to count is fine,
but teaching kids what counts is
best."

— Bob Talbert

There are a few things in the world on which we all agree, but one area where there is little debate is that every teacher is a superhero. Teachers play a crucial role in shaping the minds and futures of their students. Each teacher brings their own set of experiences, talents, and perspectives to the classroom, making them unique and impactful in their own ways.

Like all superheroes, teachers are dedicated to their mission of imparting knowledge and helping students grow. They often go above and beyond their duties to ensure the success and well-being of their students. They are able to impart learning in ways that reach their students.

Teachers use their powers to inspire and empower their students. They instill confidence, encourage critical thinking, and motivate them to pursue their dreams. And, just like superheroes face villains, teachers face diverse challenges, especially because they encounter a wide range of students with different needs and learning styles. They must adapt their teaching methods and use various resources to cater to each student effectively.

But that's not all, teachers have to often think on their feet as they encounter numerous obstacles in the classroom, such as managing behavior, addressing individual learning needs, and handling unexpected situations. They use their creativity and problem-solving skills to find solutions and maintain a positive learning environment.

Perhaps your greatest skill is your ability to create a safe and supportive space where students feel comfortable expressing themselves and growing as individuals. It is for this reason and all the others I have mentioned that teachers can have a lasting impact on their students' lives, influencing their choices, beliefs, and career paths long after they leave the classroom. They often inspire a growth mindset in their students, encouraging them to embrace challenges and view failures as opportunities for learning and improvement.

All the while teachers must promote diversity and inclusion by celebrating the uniqueness of each student and fostering an environment where everyone feels valued and respected. This means that there are times when teachers must advocate for a particular student and play a vital role in shaping education policies and curriculum development that help the school at large.

It seems obvious to most that teachers contribute to shaping the future by nurturing the next generation of leaders, innovators, and change-makers. Their contributions to society cannot be underestimated — though they often are.

There is a reason I named this book *99% a Human, 1% Amazing*. That is because it is the amazing part of you we must tap into as it makes all the difference.

Our DNA, the blueprint of life, defines our humanity and makes us unique individuals. It is fascinating to learn that out of the three billion base pairs of DNA in our bodies, only a small portion—about 20,000 base pairs—make up our coding DNA, which determines our traits and characteristics. This coding DNA, our 1%, is what truly sets us apart and makes us extraordinary.

Similarly, teachers possess their own unique qualities, experiences, and talents. They play a crucial role in education, not merely for financial rewards but driven by a genuine desire to cater to their students' needs and make a difference in their lives. They are trained to handle diverse students and their individual requirements.

Just as every human shares around 99% of their DNA with others, teachers may share some commonalities in their profession. However, it is that remaining 1%— their authenticity and unique approach—that empowers them to connect with students in a way that no one else can.

I believe that every teacher has the potential to be extraordinary and positively impact their students' lives. Embracing their individuality and believing in their abilities will allow them to excel as educators. Students need their teachers' genuine selves, their 1%, to inspire, guide, and nurture them towards growth and success.

My purpose is to support teachers in achieving success sooner through practical tips, strategies, and resources. But, even more, I want to emphasize the importance of living in your 1% as a teacher. Embrace your uniqueness, be bold, be true to yourself, and bring that authentic version of you to the classroom. Your students deserve nothing less than the 100% real you, for that is what will make a lasting impact on their lives.

Encouraging educators to embrace their uniqueness, be bold, and stay true to themselves is a powerful message. As teachers, we often have the opportunity to make a profound impact on the lives of our students. And that impact is amplified when we bring our authentic selves to the classroom.

In a world where conformity can sometimes overshadow individuality, reminding teachers of the significance of their 1% is a vital call to action. Our 1% represents the essence of who we are—our passions, experiences, and perspectives that make us stand out as educators. By living in our 1%, we demonstrate to our students the power of being genuine and true to oneself.

When we show up in the classroom as the 100% real version of ourselves, we create an environment of trust and authenticity. Our students can relate to us on a deeper level, making it easier for them to connect with the subject matter and learn effectively. Remember we teach people, our students, not subjects.

Moreover, being authentic role models allows our students to feel comfortable embracing their own uniqueness and individuality.

Teaching goes beyond delivering information; it's about forming meaningful connections with our students and guiding them towards personal growth and development. By living in our 1%, we set an example of confidence and self-assurance, inspiring our students to do the same.

The goal is not only to empower teachers to be exceptional educators but also to encourage you to cultivate a positive and supportive classroom culture. It is in this space that students can thrive, learn, and discover their potential. They can tap into their 1% just as you have tapped into yours.

Remember, it's not about being a version of someone else; it's about being the best version of yourself. So, let's be confident, passionate, and genuine educators, changing lives and making a difference in the world of education. 99% of your DNA is just what makes you a human, but it's that 1% that makes you amazing. Lean into that 1% to make the difference that only you can.

Now it is your turn. Take a few moments to reflect below, to determine what is in your 1%, so that you can operate in your Zone of Excellence.

For free bonuses and a digital version of this exercise, scan the code below or visit:

www.onepercentamazing.com/resources

Reflection Worksheet

What do you do without even thinking about it that garners praise from others?

When people come to you for advice, what topics do they ask about?

What are some things that come naturally to you that seem like a challenge for others?

If I am never able to do *this thing* again, I will feel incomplete. What is that thing?

Chapter 6: Your Differences are Not Your Deficiencies

"Similarities don't allow us to make a difference, only differences do that. Similarities allow us to connect, but differences allow us to impact."

- Daryl Williams Jr.

We talk a lot about why it's important that teachers tap into that 1% that makes them unique and special, resisting the urge to conform to others. This is because your differences are what allow you to <u>make</u> a difference.

Teachers bring their own set of experiences, skills, and passions to the classroom. That's OK! By acknowledging and celebrating these differences, they can connect with students in a way that resonates with them personally. Students come from diverse backgrounds and have various learning styles, and teachers who embrace their uniqueness can tailor their approach to meet individual needs effectively.

Moreover, when teachers authentically show up as their true selves, they model self-acceptance and encourage students to do the same. This creates an inclusive and welcoming environment where students feel valued and understood. It fosters a sense of belonging and helps students embrace their own uniqueness without feeling the need to conform to societal pressures.

By leveraging their 1% of amazing, teachers can design creative and innovative lessons, incorporate their interests and passions, and inspire students to explore their own potential. These unique qualities, combined with a genuine passion for teaching, have the power to ignite a lifelong love of learning in their students.

Ultimately, it's through embracing and celebrating our differences that teachers can truly make a lasting impact on their students' lives, helping them grow into confident, compassionate, and successful individuals who are empowered to make a difference in their own unique ways. I had to learn this message for myself. I hope that from my experience, you can skip ahead and simply accept that your differences are strengths, not deficiencies.

Throughout my life, I often struggled with a deep sense of inadequacy and not feeling like I was enough. Growing up in Staten Island, New York, in an environment filled with crime and poverty, I faced numerous challenges. But perhaps not for the reasons that you may assume. Though there were terrible things happening in my zip code, I was shielded from them in my household. My home was a unique haven that was filled with love, care, and support, which directed me down a path contrary to what my neighborhood would suggest.

While I am grateful now for the way that my family shielded me from being influenced by my environment as a child, my younger self was not so appreciative. I was set up to be viewed as "the weird kid" amongst my peers because I was so different than most of them. I attended a Title 1 school with a majority of minority students, but I was academically qualified to be a part of honors classes. In these classes I was aligned academically but felt socially disconnected from my peers. Being the only black student in my class at times, I found it difficult to connect with others, despite excelling academically.

My elective classes were not homogeneously structured, which further emphasized my differences from the majority of students. Unfortunately, even in these classes filled with black and brown students, where I hoped to embrace my passion for singing, acting, and dancing, I faced ridicule and name-calling. Their favorite name to call me was "Oreo." Because from their perspective, although I was Black on the outside, I was actually White on the inside. I was teased because I "used big words," "talked weird," and ate vegetarian cuisine before it was cool.

I felt as if I was not good enough to fit in with any peer group. I couldn't wait to get out of middle school. "Surely kids will be nicer to me in High School," I thought. However, these feelings of inadequacy persisted through high school, and college, leading me to constantly question my identity and worth. However, I later realized that I was measuring myself using the wrong standards—the ones set by others.

The turning point came when I chose to embrace my uniqueness and recognize that my differences were not deficiencies but attributes that made me amazing. It dawned on me that I am the only person on this planet who can be me, and that is my true strength.

The pivotal moment in my life occurred when I made the conscious decision to fully embrace my uniqueness and acknowledge that my differences were not shortcomings but rather extraordinary attributes that made me truly amazing. It was an enlightening realization that transformed my perspective and empowered me to embrace my individuality without reservations.

I came to understand that being myself was not just acceptable, but it was my ultimate strength. I realized that I am the only person on this vast planet who can be me, with my own set of experiences, skills, and passions. This inherent uniqueness is something no one else can replicate, and that realization was liberating.

The moment I embraced my true self, I felt a profound sense of freedom and authenticity. I no longer had to pretend to be someone I wasn't or mold myself to fit into other people's expectations. Instead, I could confidently stand tall, knowing that my differences were my strengths.

Rather than viewing my differences as deficiencies, I began to see them as my superpowers. Once known as the kid who "talks weird," I now use my voice an communication skills to empower millions of people across the globe. Through student empowerment assemblies, staff professional development sessions, district keynotes, and content on social media, my voice has become a huge way through which I impact. Each aspect of my identity, no matter how seemingly insignificant, contributed to the tapestry of my character. I had unique perspectives, talents, and insights to offer the world, and these qualities made me an invaluable asset.

This newfound understanding encouraged me to celebrate my uniqueness, cherishing the qualities that set me apart from others. It allowed me to break free from the chains of self-doubt and self-criticism, recognizing that the essence of who I am is a source of power and potential.

Embracing my individuality not only elevated my self-esteem but also profoundly impacted how I interacted with others. I noticed that my genuine authenticity resonated with people on a deeper level. Instead of trying to fit in, I allowed myself to stand out. In so doing, I could connect with others from a place of sincerity and openness.

Furthermore, embracing my uniqueness had a ripple effect on those around me. As a teacher, I saw how my students responded positively to me. They could trust me more because I was being the real me. They felt more comfortable being themselves, knowing that their teacher celebrated and valued individuality.

Today, I continue to embrace my uniqueness and encourage others to do the same. I firmly believe that our differences are not barriers but bridges to understanding and growth.

Each of us has a distinct story to tell and a unique contribution to make. By honoring and celebrating our individuality, we unlock the power to create a more diverse and exciting world. Stand tall in your authenticity and proclaim, "I am amazing because I am me."

I want to share this important message with everyone, especially educators. Despite the challenges we may face, it's crucial to identify and celebrate our 1%—the qualities and perspectives that make us unique and exceptional.

I urge you to acknowledge your differences, discover what makes you amazing, and release yourself from the wrong standards set by others. Stand tall and live out loud, unapologetically embracing your unique teaching style, your personality and the role you were destined to play in the educational community.

Remember that 99% may be common to all humans, but it's that 1%—the amazing you—that will make all the difference. Embrace your uniqueness and empower yourself to inspire greatness in your life and the lives of your students.

I came to a powerful realization that life is too short to live it according to someone else's expectations. I decided to take control and make a turn in my life. No longer would I let others' opinions dictate how I should show up or define my worth. The turning point occurred when I understood that my feelings of inadequacy stemmed from measuring myself against the wrong standards.

I often share a story about my sister making a shirt for me that I really wanted to wear but never could. She sewed a shirt for me from scratch, and it had a nice look and feel, but it didn't fit. I squeezed into it, but I was extremely uncomfortable. It squeezed my chest, made it hard to breathe, and my relaxed arms looked like the hands of clock showing 4:40. I asked her where she got the measurements for the shirt from. She revealed that she used a shirt from the pile in my room as the standard. I chuckled because she had no idea that the pile that she pulled from was clothes that I was donating because they no longer fit me. Unfortunately, she created something that was functional and beautiful; but it didn't work for me. It humorously illustrates that using the wrong standard to measure ourselves can lead to discomfort and feelings of inadequacy. The key to overcoming this is to stop measuring yourself against a standard that wasn't made for you. We must learn how to recognize and accept our differences, knowing they are not deficiencies but unique attributes that shape our destiny.

I encourage everyone to own up to their differences and recognize that they are amazing just as they are. Each person is the only expert in their own experience, and embracing their uniqueness with confidence will allow them to make a difference in the world. Life may not always be easy or perfect, but rather than chasing a fantasy of perfection, we should celebrate the beauty in our individual realities. It's essential to acknowledge the challenges, emotions, and struggles students face, ensuring we meet them where they are and support them through their unique journeys.

A fantasy says that this career will be easy all the time. It's essential to recognize that though you don't have a perfect fantasy, there's beauty in your reality. When students are not exactly where we want them to be yet, find beauty in the fact that thanks to your efforts, they have come a long way from where they used to be. Your love, care, and support are changing their lives and leaving a lasting impact that they will always remember, and that's beautiful.

Rather than getting caught up in a perfect fantasy, it's vital to embrace the beauty in your reality. Remember that your unique differences set you apart and make you amazing. Don't be afraid to stand out and embrace those aspects that make you who you are.

Every person on this Earth is different and unique. Despite 99% of our DNA being the same as everyone else, it's the 1% that makes us extraordinary. Embrace that 1% and be your amazing self, living the life you choose instead of settling for anything less. Don't let anyone else's viewpoint dictate how you should show up in the world. You are the lead singer in your life; stop singing backup. It's time to grab the mic, take center stage, and shine brightly.

The stakes are high. You make the difference. With your unique contribution, we can reach the goal where every student gets to live the life they choose, not the life they are forced to settle for.

Chapter 7: Run Your Race

"I touch the future. I teach."

– Christa McAuliffe

Dreams are the seeds of possibility that take root in the fertile soil of our imagination. They are the visions that inspire us to reach for the stars, to transcend the ordinary, and to believe in the extraordinary. Dreams are the material from which we craft reality.

In the realm of dreams, there are no boundaries, no limitations. We can soar beyond the confines of reality, exploring uncharted territories of our minds and hearts. Dreams fuel our passions, igniting the flames of ambition within us, and propelling us towards the realization of our deepest desires.

But do we dare to dream?

Remembering to Dream

Rekindling the art of dreaming can be a transformative and empowering experience. It starts with giving yourself permission, without judgment or limitations. Give your mind the freedom to explore new possibilities and envision a future in teaching that excites and motivates you.

Reconnect with your passions and reflect on the activities or interests that brought you joy and excitement in the past. Revisiting these passions can spark new dreams and aspirations aligned with your authentic self.

My recommendation is that you set aside time for daydreaming. In our fast-paced lives, we often neglect moments of contemplation and imagination. We don't pause long enough to visualize our ideal teaching situation. Take time to visualize the life you desire, incorporating both personal and professional aspects. Creating mental images of your dreams can help solidify your intentions and provide a roadmap for your journey.

I would even go so far as to writing your dreams down. Putting your dreams into words can give them clarity and substance. Journaling or creating vision boards can be powerful tools to manifest your aspirations. You might even find a trusted friend or mentor to communicate your dreams to. Verbalizing your aspirations can strengthen your commitment and make them feel more tangible.

As you dream, it may be necessary to break them down. Divide your dreams into smaller, achievable goals. This approach helps you create a step-by-step plan and provides a sense of progress as you accomplish each milestone. As you plan, remember to stay curious and open-minded about the world around you. Explore new experiences, seek inspiration from others, and be receptive to unexpected opportunities.

Keep in mind that there are dream-slayers afoot. Be sure to surround yourself with positivity. Positive people who support and encourage your dreams are influences that can uplift your spirits and motivate you to stay focused on your aspirations.

Another dream killer is the fear of failure. Fear of failure can hinder our ability to dream big. Embrace the idea that setbacks are part of the journey and view them as learning experiences rather than roadblocks. If you stay persistent in the face of difficulty, it will bring you closer to achieving dreams that might not happen overnight. Stay committed and persistent, knowing that every small step moves you closer to your goals.

Be sure to celebrate progress. Acknowledge and celebrate even the smallest achievements along the way. Each success is a testament to your commitment and determination.

Remember, dreaming is not just for the young; it's helpful in our lives at any stage. As we chase our dreams, we uncover hidden talents, untapped potential, and a reservoir of resilience we never knew existed. The pursuit of our dreams reveals the depths of our character and the unwavering spirit that lies inside of us.

Dreams are not meant to be idle fantasies but the catalysts of action. They beckon us to step out of our comfort zones and venture into the unknown. They call us to take risks, embrace change, and seize opportunities that lead us closer to our aspirations.

Yet, in the pursuit of our dreams, we must remember that the journey is just as significant as the destination. We can't get so focused on the goal that we miss the magic of getting there. Along the way, we forge relationships, build memories, and learn life's invaluable lessons.

Align Your Dreams

Aligning your dreams to your abilities is a powerful approach that ensures your aspirations are grounded in realism and attainable progress. While it's essential to have ambitious dreams that challenge and motivate you, it's equally crucial to recognize your current skills, strengths, and limitations. By aligning your dreams with your abilities, you can create a clear and practical path towards achieving your goals. It all begins by understanding your unique set of abilities, talents, and experiences. Reflect on your past achievements, interests, and areas where you excel. Spend some time with this activity to be sure you tap into even the areas you might deem insignificant. Recognize your strengths and acknowledge any areas where you might need improvement. This self-awareness will provide a solid foundation for aligning your dreams with your capabilities.

The turning point in my journey arrived when I did this. I wholeheartedly embraced my uniqueness and shed the belief that I had to conform to others. It was an awakening that revealed to me that my differences were not deficiencies, but rather attributes that made me genuinely amazing. Understanding that no one else on this planet could be me was my true source of strength.

Initially, I found myself attempting to emulate the strategies of other educators, thinking that it would lead to success. Sometimes, I even believed that just showing up as a black male educator in a predominantly black school would automatically garner gratitude and appreciation. However, reality proved different, and I faced challenges that made me question my worth.

It dawned on me that being comfortable in my own skin and walking in my purpose were the keys to breaking free from this cycle. I came to a profound realization that my path was unique, and trying to be like everyone else was futile. This understanding allowed me to embrace my authenticity, recognizing that my true potential lay in running my own race.

To illustrate this point to my students, I often use track and field analogies. On my track team, I encourage students to try various events before settling on one that aligns with their talents and passions. Each event requires a different strategy to succeed. For instance, the 100-meter dash demands an explosive start, maintaining strength throughout, and a powerful finish. In contrast, running the mile requires a safe and smart pace to sustain energy throughout the distance.

Similarly, life offers various races for each of us to run. There is no need to compare ourselves to others or mimic their strategies. Our success lies in identifying our unique races and devising the right strategies that suit our strengths and aspirations. Just like Olympic athletes competing in different events, we must focus on our race and run it with everything we have.

This is exactly what Conan O'Brien had to learn. Regarded now as one of the greatest comedians and talk show hosts of his generation, Conan knows what it is like to struggle to run his own race. In a commencement speech at Dartmouth College in 2011, he tells a story of his path in comedy. He talks about wanting to be just like David Letterman, or Johnny Carson, and failing at it. He then talks about why he is so grateful that he failed. My favorite quote from that speech is when he said, "It is our failure to become our perceived ideal that ultimately defines us and makes us unique." Failing at being David Letterman, is what made him Conan O'Brien.

In the classroom and in life, we should not be consumed by what others are doing or comparing ourselves to their achievements. Our primary competition should be with ourselves. Success is not about comparing ourselves to anybody else. It is about what we do compared to what we are capable of doing. When you max out your potential, then you've been successful.

Therefore, I encourage you to be confident in being your 1% self – that unique individual who brings something extraordinary to the world. Recognize that the pursuit of excellence is not an exception but an expectation. By running your race with authenticity and determination, you can make a difference and realize that you are more than enough. So, stay true to yourself and embrace the journey that only you can run.

Dare To Dream

Dare to dream, for dreams are the seeds of possibility that take root in the fertile soil of our imagination. They are the visions that inspire us to reach for the stars, to transcend the ordinary, and to believe in the extraordinary.

In the realm of dreams, there are no boundaries, no limitations. It is a world where we can soar beyond the confines of reality, exploring uncharted territories of our minds and hearts. Dreams fuel our passions, ignite the flames of ambition within us, and propel us towards the realization of our deepest desires.

But do we dare? The foundation of dreaming is courage. It takes courage to embrace the visions that seem distant and unattainable. It demands that we confront our fears, doubts, and insecurities. Yet, it is precisely this audacity to dream that separates those who merely exist from those who truly live.

Courage will push us past obstacles and setbacks that test our resolve. But even in moments of uncertainty, our dreams become the North Star to guide us. Courage is what keeps our eyes on our purpose, giving us the strength to persevere and the tenacity to push forward.

So, dare to dream with unyielding determination. Embrace the uncertainty, for therein lies the excitement of discovery. Let your dreams soar high and be unwavering in your pursuit.

One of my favorite responses ever given in the history of mankind, was given by Mike Vance, a friend of Walt Disney. The Florida Disney World Amusement Park was completed and opened four years after Walt Disney passed away. Right after opening, an onlooker stood in awe as he gazed over the vast incredible creation and said to Mike Vance, "Isn't it too bad Walt Disney didn't live to see this?" Mike Vance replied, He did see it-that's why it's here!"

You've got to dream it, before you can be it.

Chapter 8: Creating a Classroom Theme that Fits Your Vision

"I never teach my pupils; I only attempt to provide the conditions in which they can learn."

— Albert Einstein

Rather than spending time scrolling on YouTube, Facebook, Instagram, or TikTok, comparing and borrowing other teachers' classroom decorating ideas, accept the challenge of creating a unique and exciting classroom theme of your own!

I believe in maximizing student growth and one of the ways you can do it is by redesigning your own classroom theme. Trust me when I assure you that it's much more fulfilling than simply adopting someone else's.

Certainly, it's a great idea to gather inspiration from other teachers' themes. For instance, perhaps there is a middle school math teacher who has a clean and well-organized classroom that you might find appealing. Similarly, maybe there is an elementary teacher who brings vibrant colors and a positive vibe to her space. Instead of copying other people's themes outright, figure out how to make it your own.

It All Starts with a Vision

The first step is to start with a vision. Revisit the vision that you set in Chapter 2. Having a clear and captivating vision for your classroom theme is essential in creating an exciting and inspiring learning environment. Your vision serves as the guiding light, driving your creativity and shaping the overall atmosphere of the classroom.

Start by considering your teaching philosophy and the goals you have for your students. Think about the values and principles that define your teaching style. Your classroom theme should align with these beliefs and support your teaching objectives.

Before you finalize your plan, get to know your students and their interests. Understand their diverse backgrounds, hobbies, and passions. By incorporating elements that resonate with your students, you can create a more engaging and inclusive environment. If you insist on having your theme ready on the first day of school, send "getting to know you sheets" to parents before school or talk to students and parents at pre-term events.

Brainstorm themes before deciding. Have a good plan? Set it aside and come up with another one. Let your imagination run wild and brainstorm various themes that you believe would ignite excitement among your students. Consider themes related to nature, space, literature, history, or any subject that fascinates both you and your students. Then compare your plans to see which is best of what elements of each you want to use.

Consider Your Objectives

Define specific objectives you want to achieve with your classroom theme. Whether it's fostering creativity, encouraging collaboration, or promoting a growth mindset, your theme should serve a purpose beyond mere decoration. You might even collaborate with colleagues who are more creative or who have great skill at bringing your vision to life. You don't want to copy them. You want them to assist in your idea. Collaborating with others can provide valuable insights and fresh perspectives, helping you refine your vision.

Considering your objectives helps you remain consistent and authentic. While seeking inspiration from others is valuable, ensure that your vision is authentic and unique to you and your students. Infuse your personality and teaching style into the theme to create a genuine and memorable experience.

Share your vision with students, parents, and colleagues to gather feedback. Their input can offer valuable suggestions and help refine your ideas. You might have an amazing parent whose skills and "eye" are invaluable to you.

Just stay flexible. Remember that a vision is not cast in stone. Embrace the opportunity to adapt and refine your theme as the school year progresses and new ideas emerge.

A well-crafted vision for your classroom theme goes beyond aesthetics. It shapes the learning experience, fosters a positive and enthusiastic atmosphere, and leaves a lasting impression on your students. With a strong vision in place, you can create an exciting and engaging learning environment that supports academic growth and personal development.

Consider your students' interests as well. Your classroom should be a comfortable and inviting space for them. Think about their demographics, age-appropriateness, and likes when planning your theme. That's one good reason to wait until after the school year begins or gather data in advance.

Think About Budget

Establish a budget for your classroom theme. Decide how much money you're comfortable spending to bring your vision to life. As you develop your vision, consider factors such as classroom layout, available space, and safety measures. A vision that is both inspiring and feasible will make it easier to execute.

Creating a budget for your classroom theme is a critical step in bringing your vision to life. It allows you to allocate your resources wisely and make intentional decisions about how to transform your classroom space. Consider it a financial roadmap that will guide you in achieving your goals without stretching yourself too thin.

To begin, take some time to assess your available funds. Consider any personal contributions you're willing to make and explore potential sources of funding, such as grants or school budgets. I personally like to make my own wallet the last option. I believe that when you intentionally remove options, you are forced to get creative and find new ones. When I told myself to stop spending on my classroom, I then found organizations, sponsors, and school funds to donate. I received more, while contributing less.

Remember, your vision is the driving force behind your classroom theme. As you plan your budget, keep your vision at the forefront of your decisions. Prioritize the elements that align most closely with your goals and the needs of your students. Just because it is cute, doesn't mean you need it in your class. Think about the materials, decorations, and resources that will best support your teaching objectives while staying within your financial boundaries.

Consider seeking cost-effective alternatives for certain items. Look for deals, discounts, or repurpose materials creatively to stretch your budget further. Keep in mind that simplicity can often be just as effective as extravagance. It's not about how much money you spend, but how you strategically invest it to enhance the learning experience for your students.

Additionally, involving your students and their families in the budgeting process can foster a sense of ownership and community. Engage them in discussions about the classroom theme and its potential expenses. This not only demonstrates transparency but also instills a sense of responsibility among students to take care of their learning environment.

As you make budgetary decisions, be flexible and open to adjustments. Sometimes, unforeseen circumstances or opportunities may arise that require you to tweak your initial plans. Being adaptable will allow you to make the most of your budget and ensure that your classroom theme remains aligned with your vision.

By establishing a well-thought-out budget, you can confidently embark on creating a captivating and inspiring classroom environment that reflects your unique vision. Remember, it's not about the amount you spend, but the purposeful choices you make to enhance the educational journey of your students.

Match Your Style

Don't forget about your preferences. Since you'll be consistent with the theme, make sure it aligns with your taste and style. You should be excited to talk about it, share it with others, and feel comfortable with it throughout the year.

To make your theme catchy, consider alliteration or rhyming. People love memorable phrases, and this will add a fun element to your theme.

When it comes to colors and patterns, keep it simple. Stick to two to three colors or patterns to create a consistent and branded look for your classroom.

By following these steps, you'll create a unique and personalized classroom theme that fosters a positive learning environment and keeps everyone invested and engaged.

For free bonuses and a digital version of this exercise, scan the code below or visit:

www.onepercentamazing.com/resources

Chapter 9: Good Teachers Teach Subjects, Great Teachers Teach Students

"Educating the mind without educating the heart is no education at all."

-Aristotle

Standards are important. We are all bound by them, measured by them, and contracted to pay attention to them. However, standards in education are not everything. In fact, they are not even the most important thing.

While teaching standards undeniably play a crucial role in education, it is essential to recognize that they are not the sole determinant of effective teaching and student success. True, they provide a common framework and guidelines for what students should know and be able to do at specific grade levels. However, it is equally critical to understand that standards do not encompass the entirety of education's purpose. They should not overshadow other essential aspects of teaching and learning that foster holistic development and prepare students for life beyond the classroom.

Education is not just about meeting a checklist of standards and ticking off learning objectives. It goes beyond the mere transmission of knowledge. True education involves shaping young minds, nurturing their curiosity, and instilling in them a love for learning that extends beyond the classroom walls.

The most important aspect of education is the student. Each child is unique, with diverse strengths, talents, and aspirations. As educators, our primary responsibility is to cater to the individual needs of our students, recognizing that not every child learns the same way or at the same pace. We must create an inclusive, supportive, and engaging learning environment that encourages students to thrive.

Teaching should empower students to think critically, problem-solve, communicate effectively, and collaborate with others. These skills, often referred to as "21st-century skills," are invaluable in navigating the complexities of the modern world and preparing students for future success.

Moreover, education is not just about academic achievement; it's about becoming a learner. When students develop from passive hearers to active learners, a critical character development milestone is reached. We move them from the back seat to the driver's seat as they take the reins of their own learning. Additionally, we hope to instill values such as work ethic, empathy, compassion, integrity, and resilience in our students, helping them become not only knowledgeable individuals but also responsible and ethical citizens.

In the pursuit of excellence in education, we must look beyond the confines of standardized testing and grades. We should focus on fostering a love for learning, encouraging curiosity, and inspiring students to become lifelong learners, something that will take them into the future, setting them up for success. A well-rounded education should ignite a passion for exploration and creativity, fostering a sense of wonder and an insatiable thirst for knowledge.

The current model of teaching derives from the days when factories were new and on the rise. But is that model still the best for students today? Memorization, rote learning, and spitting back facts we spat at them is not enough to compete in today's world.

In today's world, it isn't enough to do your job well; you must be indispensable.

> *"The linchpins among us are not the ones born with a magical talent. No, they are people who have decided that a new kind of work is important, and trained themselves to do it... The only way to get what you're worth is to stand out, to exert emotional labor, to be seen as indispensable,*

and to produce interactions that
organizations and people care
deeply about."
— *Seth Godin (Author), Linchpin:*
Are You Indispensable?

Ultimately, while standards provide a structure for educational goals, it is the art of teaching that transforms students' lives. Great teachers go beyond the curriculum, incorporating real-world experiences, hands-on learning, and critical thinking opportunities. They connect with their students on a personal level, understanding their strengths and challenges, and provide the necessary support to help them thrive.

We can never discount or forget that the heart of education lies in nurturing the potential of every student, creating a profound impact on their lives, and empowering them to become active, responsible, and compassionate contributors to society.

Think about popular fast-food chains like McDonald's and Chick-fil-A. While both provide food, Chick-fil-A stands out with its exceptional customer service, quality food, and an experience that leaves customers feeling valued and satisfied. If the McDonald's line is long, you'll probably keep driving and look for something else. If the Chick-fil-A line is out of the parking lot, you'll probably get on the back of the line, get comfortable in the seat, and text your team that you're running behind this morning. Chick-fil-A understands that it's not just about getting the job done; it's about creating a life-changing experience.

Now, let's apply this analogy to education. As teachers, you can simply focus on delivering subject content, and that's important. But it's not enough to "pursue the pacing guide" when students also need to be taught how to prioritize. It's not enough to just "cultivate the content" when students also need to be taught how to communicate confidently. It's not enough to just "stick to the standards" when students also need to know how to stand for what matters. But to be a transformational teacher, one who truly changes lives, you must go beyond just teaching subjects. Great teachers recognize that students matter the most. Good teachers teach subjects, great teachers teach students.

Teaching students life skills is crucial in preparing them for success, not just in your classroom but throughout their lives. Life skills encompass stress management, time management, budgeting, conflict resolution, and much more. These skills empower students to navigate the challenges they'll face in the real world and build the foundation for successful human beings.

We became educators to make a difference, and while topics like the quadratic formula have their place, teaching life skills is equally essential. Consider this: How often will students use the quadratic formula outside of school? Not as frequently as they'll need life skills like managing stress, resolving conflicts, and managing time effectively.

Let's be clear; teaching life skills doesn't mean neglecting content and state standards. It's about blending subject matter with practical skills. It's about empowering students with the ability to apply the knowledge they acquire, fostering critical thinking, and helping them become well-rounded individuals.

Your instruction can give students enough to pass a class or ace a test, but to change lives, you must equip them with essential life skills. These skills are what will make a difference in their lives when they face challenges and difficult times.

As educators, we must shift our perspective and see teaching as an opportunity to provide students with more than just academic knowledge. We have the power to influence mindset development, build character, and teach life skills that will resonate with them beyond the classroom, shaping their futures and changing our world.

SECTION 3
Ignore Your Doubters

Chapter 10: Jumping Hurdles

"Life is often compared to a marathon, but I think it is more like being a sprinter: Long stretches of hard work punctuated by brief moments in which we are given the opportunity to perform at our best."

—Michael Johnson, Olympic track star

Doubters will say that you can't make an impact because there are too many hurdles in your way. Ignore them.

Ignoring your doubters is undoubtedly easier said than done. While it may sound like a straightforward concept in theory, putting it into practice can be a challenging task. Doubtful voices can be persistent, echoing in the back of your mind, questioning your decisions and abilities. These doubts can seep into your thoughts, causing insecurities and uncertainties about your chosen path.

Moreover, the emotional toll of disregarding negative opinions from colleagues, parents, or superiors can be overwhelming, especially if their doubts come from a place of genuine concern.

Human nature tends to seek validation and approval, making it difficult to completely shut out the disapproval of others. Additionally, societal pressure and fear of failure can intensify the impact of doubters' remarks.

To truly ignore your doubters takes immense inner strength, unwavering self-confidence, and a determination to stay focused on your goals, regardless of external criticism. It is a journey of personal growth and resilience, requiring constant self-assessment and the ability to differentiate between constructive feedback and baseless negativity.

Nevertheless, mastering the art of ignoring doubters can lead to a greater sense of self-belief and empowerment in pursuing your dreams and achieving success on your terms. Throughout the next six chapters, we will talk about how to implement strategies that will help you rise above the negativity of doubters. You have to keep going over the first wave of doubt knowing that another wave is soon to come. It's much like jumping hurdles.

Hurdle jumpers cannot miss a single barrier. They must jump over every one. That's the rule of the game. Miss one and the race is not won. The good news is that it doesn't matter how poorly you jump the hurdle. You might fall over it, kick it as you sail over, or even knock it down. So long as you get past it. Teaching is just like jumping hurdles.

Teaching requires the ability to overcome challenges and obstacles with determination and precision. In the race of education, teachers are the hurdle jumpers, guiding their students toward success. Just as the hurdler must navigate each hurdle flawlessly, educators cannot afford to miss a single opportunity to inspire, educate, and empower their students.

In the journey of teaching, every student's growth and development matters. Each hurdle represents a unique learning moment, and teachers must ensure that their students overcome every one of them. The race is not won if we refuse to push hard enough to get over a few hurdles; it's about helping every student progress and achieve their full potential.

Teaching, like hurdling, demands persistence and resilience. But what matters most is the unwavering commitment to get past each challenge. We've covered a lot about commitment — for good reason. As a teacher, it's crucial to provide support and encouragement, helping students rise above their difficulties and build the confidence to keep going. And our message to keep going is lost if we quit as teachers.

Additionally, the process of teaching, like hurdling, requires a careful balance of strategy and adaptability. Hurdle jumpers must adjust their approach based on their speed, technique, and the distance between the hurdles. Similarly, educators must tailor their teaching methods to cater to the individual needs, strengths, and weaknesses of their students. One size does not fit all, and teachers must be flexible in their instructional approaches.

Ultimately, the analogy of teaching as hurdle jumping emphasizes the responsibility and dedication teachers have in shaping young minds and empowering the next generation. Like the skilled hurdler, teachers must leap over challenges, guide their students with precision and care, and ensure that every hurdle is cleared, one by one. By doing so, they create a foundation for future success and a brighter future for their students.

Hurdle Number 1 – The Students

Moreover, just as a hurdler can't miss a hurdle, an educator's true success lies in ensuring that every student achieves academic, emotional, and personal growth. It's not enough for a few students to excel while others struggle. Effective teaching means equipping all students with the tools they need to thrive and reach their goals.

At times, while striving to support and assist students, educators encounter a unique challenge - the students themselves inadvertently obstructing the learning process. It may seem paradoxical, as the primary goal of teaching is to facilitate student growth and development. However, various factors can contribute to this situation, requiring a delicate approach to navigate and address these obstacles effectively.

One possible reason for students getting in their own way is the fear of failure. The pressure to perform well academically or socially can lead some students to adopt self-sabotaging behaviors. They may become apprehensive about taking risks, fearing that any misstep could result in disappointment or judgment from others. As a result, they might procrastinate, avoid challenging tasks, or not put in their full effort, hindering their own progress.

Another factor contributing to this issue is the lack of self-belief and confidence. Some students may struggle with low self-esteem, doubting their abilities or feeling unworthy of success. These feelings of inadequacy can create a self-fulfilling prophecy, leading them to underperform and miss out on opportunities for growth and achievement.

In some cases, students may inadvertently undermine their own learning by exhibiting disruptive or attention-seeking behaviors. These actions may be a manifestation of underlying emotional or behavioral challenges, requiring the teacher's understanding and support to address effectively.

Many students come to school with much more than their books, pencils, and a peanut butter and jelly sandwich for lunch. Some come with adult-sized burdens.

I am reminded of the time a student was in my office on the one-year anniversary of his father fatally shooting his mother in front of him. I went into the classroom on an unrelated assignment, and as I was leaving, he asked if he could come with me. I was enroute to complete another task and was prepared to deny his request, but his eyes said that he needed to talk. "One lap," I said to him, signifying that we could take one lap around the building, and then we would return to class.

He lit up and followed me out of the classroom. In the hallway, I asked him what was going on, and he poured out his emotions. He told me how a year ago on that day his mother and father were arguing in front of him and his two siblings when things took a turn. His father pulled out a gun and shot his mother in the head. The father then turned to the children and told them to get in the car. Leaving the mother lifeless in the bedroom, he drove the children to their Grandparent's house, and dropped them off. That would be the last time he saw either of his parents.

As he told me this story, I became overwhelmed with emotion, and that "one lap" turned into an extended stay in my office. I knew that he was missing his math block, but I also knew that he had a problem that base-ten blocks couldn't solve. We spoke for a while, and one thing he said struck a chord that will ring in my brain forever. I asked how he was feeling about everything, and he said, "I am just glad I got to spend six years with her. She was a great Mom." He was carrying all that weight on his seven-year-old shoulders, and we expected him to just sit in a class and learn.

As educators, recognizing these patterns and understanding the underlying causes is crucial. Instead of becoming frustrated or dismissing students as uncooperative, teachers can adopt a compassionate and patient approach. By fostering a safe and supportive learning environment, educators can encourage students to express their concerns and fears openly. Through active listening and empathy, teachers can help students overcome self-doubt and develop a growth mindset.

Furthermore, providing constructive feedback and recognizing students' efforts, no matter how small, can boost their self-confidence and motivate them to take on challenges with greater determination. Encouraging a positive classroom culture, where students support and uplift one another, can also counteract self-sabotaging behaviors.

Moreover, incorporating activities that foster self-awareness, strong communication skills, and emotional intelligence can be beneficial. Encouraging reflection on personal strengths and areas for growth helps students develop a deeper understanding of themselves and their abilities. This newfound awareness can empower them to take ownership of their learning journey and navigate potential hurdles more effectively.

As teachers, it is essential to strike a balance between providing guidance and allowing students the space to learn from their mistakes. Encouraging a growth mindset helps students view challenges as opportunities for learning and growth, rather than obstacles to be feared.

While it may seem counterintuitive, teachers can encounter situations where students unknowingly impede their own progress. However, by approaching these challenges with empathy, understanding, and a commitment to fostering a growth mindset, educators can help students overcome their barriers and pave the way for greater success and fulfillment in their learning journey.

Hurdle Number 2 – Other Teachers

As an ambitious and dedicated teacher striving to go above and beyond for your students, you may encounter obstacles from other educators who, for various reasons, seem to stand in your way. It can be disheartening and challenging to face criticism, backbiting, gossip, or lack of collaboration from your fellow teachers. However, it's essential to understand the underlying dynamics and potential reasons behind such behaviors and to navigate these situations with professionalism and grace.

One possible reason for this negative behavior could be insecurity and fear of comparison. When a teacher sees a colleague going the extra mile and receiving recognition or praise for their efforts, it may trigger feelings of inadequacy or jealousy. This can lead to subtle or overt criticism or gossip as a way to cope with these emotions. In such instances, it's crucial to remember that the actions of others are not a reflection of your worth or dedication as an educator.

Another factor could be a difference in teaching philosophies or approaches. Every teacher has their unique style and preferences when it comes to lesson planning, classroom management, and instructional methods. When someone encounters a colleague who differs significantly in their approach, there might be resistance or refusal to collaborate, stemming from a desire to maintain their own way of doing things.

Additionally, workplace culture and dynamics can also play a significant role in shaping interactions between teachers. If there are underlying tensions or a lack of open communication within the faculty, it can create an environment where backbiting and gossip thrive. In such cases, building strong relationships and fostering a positive school culture can help alleviate such behaviors over time.

To navigate these challenging situations, it's essential to prioritize professionalism, empathy, and open communication. Rather than engaging in conflicts or retaliating, seek to understand the perspectives of your colleagues and be receptive to feedback, even if it's delivered in a less-than-constructive manner.

Collaborating with others can be incredibly rewarding, so if a fellow teacher is hesitant to work together, consider finding common ground or shared goals that can lead to meaningful collaboration. By focusing on what you can learn from each other and how you can collectively benefit the students, you can create a more positive and productive working relationship. Offer to help rather than offer to be helped to start the process of breaking the ice.

Furthermore, seeking support and mentorship from other educators who appreciate your dedication and enthusiasm can be invaluable. Building a network of like-minded colleagues can provide encouragement and validation for your efforts.

Hurdle Number 3 – The Principal and Administration

Throughout the first two sections of this book, I encouraged you to identify your dream and illuminate your differences. I know that those are keys to unlocking your maximum impact in the classroom. There are others who may not yet be convinced – and they just might be your administrator.

As a teacher with a passion for daring to try something new in your classroom, you might encounter resistance or roadblocks from various levels of leadership, including your principal, district administrators, or other educational leaders. This situation can be frustrating and demotivating, but it's essential to navigate it with tact and perseverance to continue providing the best possible learning experience for your students.

One reason for such resistance could be a preference for the status quo or a risk-averse mindset among some leaders. Educational institutions, especially larger school districts, often have established protocols, curricula, and teaching methods that have been deemed effective over time. When a teacher proposes something new or unconventional, it might challenge these established practices and create uncertainty or apprehension among leaders.

Furthermore, leaders may also face pressure from external stakeholders, such as parents, school boards, or government bodies, which can influence decision-making processes. If an innovative approach or new idea is perceived as too risky or not aligned with the expectations of these stakeholders, leaders may hesitate to support it.

To navigate these situations effectively, communication and collaboration are key. Here are some strategies to consider:

Present a well-researched plan:

Before proposing any new initiatives, ensure you have thoroughly researched and planned the approach. Provide evidence-based support for the potential benefits and outcomes. A well-prepared and thought-out proposal can instill confidence in your leadership.

Build alliances:

Seek support from colleagues, parents, and other teachers who share your vision. Creating a network of allies can demonstrate that your idea has broader support and can mitigate concerns about its potential success. It's easy to ignore an ant; it's hard to ignore a colony.

Address concerns proactively:

Anticipate and address potential concerns or objections that leaders may have. Presenting a comprehensive plan that addresses these concerns can increase the likelihood of gaining support.

Collaborate with colleagues:

Seek opportunities to collaborate with other teachers or departments to implement your idea on a smaller scale. Demonstrating success on a smaller level can make it easier to gain approval for a broader implementation.

Use data and evidence:

Collect data from pilot projects or research studies that support the effectiveness of your proposed approach. Data-driven decision-making can be compelling for leaders. Highlight student benefits and emphasize how your innovative idea will positively impact student learning and growth. Focusing on student outcomes can resonate with leaders who prioritize student success.

Stay persistent:

Facing resistance does not mean your idea lacks merit. Continue to be persistent and resilient in advocating for your proposal. Be open to feedback and adjust your approach as needed.

Engage in professional development:

Development opportunities to strengthen your expertise and credibility in the area of your innovation. It offers research-based knowledge as well as field work to prove an idea works. Leadership is more likely to support initiatives backed by knowledgeable and skilled teachers.

Change can be gradual in educational settings, and leaders may need time to fully understand and appreciate the value of your innovative ideas. Be patient and continue to advocate for what you believe will benefit your students' education. Ultimately, the students' success and growth should remain at the forefront of all decision-making, and as a passionate educator, your dedication to their well-being will undoubtedly make a lasting impact.

The following framework is one I created while advocating to operate in my uniqueness. Administration was not always on board with me "doing my own thing." Sometimes they needed a little convincing, and proof that my idea would be an improvement over the current system. Following these seven steps I was able to clear hurdles with the administration. Currently, as an administrator, I agree that this is a great approach.

For free bonuses and a digital version of this exercise, scan the code below or visit:

www.onepercentamazing.com/resources

1. Identify Your Zone of Excellence

We all have a Zone of Excellence, or skills in our 1% that others don't do as well as us. The first step to clearing hurdles with administration is to know what lies in your Zone of Excellence. Revisit the exercise in chapter five to remind yourself of what is in your 1%.

2. Identify What is Threatening Your Zone of Excellence

The hurdle that your administration is placing in front of you is only a hurdle for you because it is threatening your Zone of Excellence. It requires you to ignore your 1% and show up inauthentically. While it is great to be stretched outside of our comfort zone, it is frustrating to be asked to refrain from utilizing the skills that make us who we are.

3. Understand the Real Reason Why They Want Things Done Their Way

While it's true that some school leaders are committed to the old model of schooling and cannot seem to open their minds to new ideas, that is not the case for all of them. Principals and administrators may have various reasons for wanting things done their way. These reasons often stem from their roles, responsibilities, and the broader context in which they operate. After all, school leaders are accountable for the overall performance of the school and its staff. They may want things done their way to ensure consistency, efficiency, and alignment with school goals and objectives. Some of that is motivated by fear of change and fear of risk, but there are other factors as well. School leaders strive to create a cohesive and unified school culture. They may have a specific vision for the school's identity and values, and want things done in a way that reflects and reinforces that vision.

It can also come down to their own limitations. Leaders often have experience and expertise in one style of education. Their approach may be based on evidence-based practices and successful strategies they have witnessed in the past. It's hard to help you flourish in your 1% when they only understand the 99%.

Let's say you are facing a classroom management hurdle because you are being asked to implement a system that doesn't align with your Zone of Excellence. Let's say the administrators are mandating that you use Class Dojo, but you have your own way of managing the class that has been effective. The real reason why they are mandating the use of Class Dojo is because they want to make sure that student behaviors are not getting in the way of student academic progress. They have experience with the efficacy of Class Dojo, and they trust the outcomes. So, knowing that this is their main focus, you can then devise a plan to prove that your idea is as effective, if not more.

4. Focus on Impacting the Areas in Which You Don't Need Permission

I do not want you to rebel. That is not the best way to go about getting what you want. It makes you look insubordinate and untrustworthy. A better course of action is to work to convince the decision makers that your idea is a viable option. The way to do that without being rebellious is to implement your idea in an area where you don't need their permission. Perhaps you try your idea with an after-school club, or in small groups, or in another element of your classroom that you have complete control over. By going this route, you aren't being a rebel, you are being a researcher.

5. Track the Data That Shows Efficacy of Your Methods Over a Period of Time

Working to convince administration is a great idea, but the method must be correct. A person convinced against their will is of their own belief still. You must convince them by presenting the information and allowing them to deduce that your idea is effective and a viable option. That means that you need data-driven evidence.

By diligently tracking and analyzing data showcasing the sustained efficacy of these methods over time, educators can build a compelling case that highlights the positive outcomes and benefits of their approaches.

One powerful tool for countering resistance is to collect quantitative data that quantifies the academic progress of students. By conducting pre- and post-assessments, educators can measure the growth in students' knowledge and skills after implementing their new teaching methods. This data can reveal significant improvements in academic performance, demonstrating the effectiveness of the approach and its positive influence on student learning outcomes.

Beyond academic performance, qualitative data can also be collected through surveys, interviews, and student feedback to gauge their engagement, motivation, and overall satisfaction with the learning experience. Capturing students' perspectives on the new methods can provide valuable insights into their effectiveness and reveal how these approaches have positively impacted their attitudes towards learning.

Moreover, data tracking should not be confined to short-term observations; sustainable efficacy requires continuous monitoring over an extended period. By maintaining consistent records and comparing data over multiple academic terms or years, educators can showcase the long-term benefits of their methods, demonstrating their potential to yield enduring positive effects on student learning and development.

Furthermore, it's crucial to establish clear objectives and align the new teaching methods with the school's overall goals and mission. When school leaders recognize that these innovative approaches contribute to achieving broader educational objectives, they are more likely to embrace and support the changes.

6. Ask to Pilot on a Larger Scale

Now that you have the data collected, present it to the administration to compare the efficacy of both strategies. If your research shows that the way they were requiring you to operate is more effective, do some self-reflection and ask yourself if you are resisting for the right reasons. If their way is more effective, but you just don't want to do it, let me remind you who we desire to impact. Students matter more than ego.

If you find that your idea is more effective, then ask to pilot some changes on a larger scale. Perhaps instead of small group implementation, you can try it with the entire class, or grade level. The term "pilot" is critical because it suggests that you are just trying it out to see if you can duplicate the success. If the pilot does not go as planned, the idea can be scrapped. If it goes well, it can become a permanent fixture. Presenting it as a pilot reduces the pressure on administrators to commit to this new idea. In most cases, if the data supports the administrator's vision, you will get a green light to pilot.

7. Do So Well They Can't Ignore You!

When you have the green light to pilot, you must duplicate or improve the data that you saw during the testing phase in step four. If you can repeat the efficacy, your idea will become a new fixture in the school. School leaders ultimately want what is best for students, and if your results are undeniably great, you will not be ignored.

Hurdle Number 4 - The Big Hurdle You Might Have Missed

One of the most significant obstacles to enacting meaningful changes within a classroom or school setting doesn't always stem from external forces like administration or other outside sources. More often than not, it is the internal fear within educators that hinders progress and innovation. Unaddressed fears can shackle our potential and keep us confined within self-imposed limitations. However, confronting and conquering these fears can liberate us, granting us the freedom to embrace transformation and inspire positive change in education.

The fear of the unknown is a common challenge that educators face when considering implementing new teaching methods or innovative approaches. It's natural to feel apprehensive about stepping into uncharted territory, unsure of how students, colleagues, and superiors will respond. Yet, it is precisely by stepping beyond our comfort zones that we can uncover new possibilities and discover untapped potential within ourselves and our students.

Another common fear is the fear of failure. We worry that our attempts at change might not yield the desired results, leading to disappointment or criticism. However, it's essential to recognize that failure is an integral part of the learning process. By embracing failure as an opportunity for growth, we can foster resilience and perseverance, setting a powerful example for our students and showing them that mistakes are steppingstones towards success.

Moreover, the fear of resistance from others, including colleagues or parents, can be daunting. The concern about facing pushback or disapproval may deter us from pursuing necessary changes. However, as educators, it is essential to remember that our primary focus should always be the well-being and growth of our students. By keeping their best interests at heart and presenting a strong rationale backed by evidence, we can build a persuasive case for the changes we seek to implement.

The fear of stepping away from traditional teaching methods might arise from a sense of attachment to familiar practices. The comfort of routines and established norms can be hard to relinquish, even when we recognize that they might not be the most effective means of fostering student learning and development. However, by embracing a growth mindset and being open to continuous improvement, we can shed these mental constraints and evolve as educators. The traditional methods used in today's classrooms are more than a hundred years. Everything has changed, so our methods must change as well. Take comfort in that.

Conquering these internal fears can lead to a sense of liberation and empowerment. When we break free from the chains of fear, we find ourselves more willing to experiment with new teaching approaches, explore innovative technologies, and engage in professional development opportunities that enrich our pedagogical skills.

Yes, the fear that holds educators back from enacting positive changes in their classrooms or schools can be a formidable obstacle. However, it is crucial to recognize that these fears are often self-imposed limitations that can be overcome. By facing our internal fears head-on and reframing them as opportunities for growth and transformation, we unlock the door to freedom—the freedom to innovate, the freedom to take risks, and the freedom to shape a vibrant and dynamic learning environment for our students. Embracing fear as a catalyst for change enables us to inspire the next generation and make a lasting impact on the future of education. The fears we don't face become our limitations. But when we fight fear, we find freedom.

Chapter 11: Share Your Vision

You cannot have a learning
organization without a shared
vision...A shared vision provides a
compass to keep learning on
course when stress develops.

—Peter Senge

Doubters will say that you can't make an impact because students won't be invested. Ignore them.

When you search for ideas on what to do on the first day of school, you'll undoubtedly come across an array of fantastic activities shared by fellow teachers. From getting-to-know-you icebreakers to growth mindset exercises, there are countless creative ideas that can set a positive tone for the start of the academic year.

However, as we immerse ourselves in the excitement of planning these engaging activities, it's crucial to remember the bigger picture. Studies have shown that many students experience nervousness and anxiety on the first day of school. As educators, we have a brief window to address these emotions and create a comforting atmosphere within our classrooms. If we focus solely on fun activities without acknowledging and alleviating students' anxieties, it might lead to lingering challenges-throughout the school year.

And it isn't just at the beginning of the school year that we should intentionally address student anxiety. According to the International Board of Credentialing and Continuing Education Standards, students grappling with anxiety tend to perform poorly academically and display erratic behavior. It's clear that fostering a positive emotional environment is vital for their success. To mitigate nervousness and anxiety, students need to know three essential things about their teacher and classroom. They need to be assured that their teacher genuinely cares about their well-being and future, that patience will be shown towards their struggles, and that the classroom is a safe space for learning and growth.

The most effective activity that encompasses all three of these crucial elements is sharing your vision with students early and often. We spoke about the fact that your vision for the class should represent what you wish to be true for every single student. It is not a specific academic goal for a certain percentage of students; instead, it is an overarching aspiration for the success, growth, and happiness of each student in your class.

By communicating your vision clearly, you show your students that they matter, that their dreams and aspirations are valued, and that you are dedicated to supporting them on their unique journey. This shared vision becomes the foundation for a cohesive and inclusive classroom community, fostering a sense of belonging and confidence among your students.

Before you can share your vision, you must craft a vision. Revisit the vision that you set in Chapter 2. Remember, your vision should be one that includes outcomes for 100% of your students.

Share your Vision with Administrators

Embarking on an exhilarating and successful school year begins with the crucial step of communicating your vision effectively to all stakeholders involved. To ensure a harmonious and productive learning environment, it's essential to share your vision with administrators, fostering a unified sense of purpose and collaboration.

First and foremost, sharing your vision with administrators lays the groundwork for a supportive and aligned educational experience. Engaging in open and transparent dialogue with school leaders allows you to articulate your aspirations, goals, and intended outcomes for the students. By involving administrators in the vision-sharing process, you demonstrate your commitment to the school's mission and objectives, fostering a sense of cohesion between your classroom and the broader educational community.

During this conversation with administrators, be sure to highlight how your vision aligns with the school's overarching goals. Emphasize the ways in which your innovative teaching methods and student-centered approach contribute to the overall growth and success of the institution. By showcasing the positive impact your vision can have on student learning and development, you build a compelling case for support and collaboration from the administrative team.

Share Your Vision with Parents

Sharing your vision with parents is a crucial step in fostering a strong partnership between home and school. Parents play a vital role in supporting their children's education, and by sharing your vision with them, you invite them to become active participants in their child's learning journey.

Clearly articulate your vision, educational philosophy, and the specific ways in which you plan to enrich their child's learning experience throughout the year. Be receptive to their questions, concerns, and feedback, as this creates an environment of mutual trust and respect.

Continuous communication with parents throughout the school year is equally essential. We will learn about this more in Chapter 19, but here's what you need to know for now. Provide regular updates on the progress of their children and involve them in classroom activities and events whenever possible. By fostering a sense of inclusion and collaboration, parents are more likely to actively support and reinforce the values and goals of your vision at home.

Expanding further, collaborating with parents allows you to gain valuable insights into the individual needs and strengths of your students. Their input can inform your instructional strategies and approaches, creating a more personalized and effective learning environment.

Share Your Vision with Students

What is it that you communicate with every single student? The effectiveness of this communication lies in its ability to address the anxiety and nervousness that some students may experience at the beginning of the school year. When you share your vision with your students, (the vision the covers 100% of your students) they know they are included, and they hear that you genuinely care about them and their future. This assurance helps to ease their anxieties, knowing that they are in an environment where they are valued and supported.

The second crucial aspect is letting your students know that you are patient with their struggles. By sharing your vision, students understand that you are not pressuring them to be perfect. Instead, they perceive that this vision is a joint effort, and you are willing to support them on their journey towards success. This knowledge fosters a sense of security and removes the fear of not being able to meet high expectations without adequate support.

Furthermore, sharing your vision with your students creates a sense of safety. They recognize that you are leading them towards a common goal and will not tolerate any behavior that hinders their progress. This assurance instills trust in you as their teacher, knowing that you will protect them from any form of bullying or harm, creating an emotionally secure learning environment.

Sharing your vision with administrators, parents, and students is a vital step in ensuring a successful and exciting school year. By engaging in open and transparent communication with school leaders, parents, and students, you align everyone's expectations and establish strong partnerships that foster a supportive and enriching learning experience for students. With everyone working together towards a shared vision, the potential for growth, learning, and success in the classroom becomes boundless.

Chapter 12: Fantasy vs. Reality

"Stop waiting for your prince to come. Go find him. Poor guy may be stuck in a tree or something."

- Anonymous

Doubters will say that you can't make an impact because your reality doesn't match their fantasy. Ignore them.

When my daughter Nyelle was 3 years old, she showed me how dangerous it can be to get lost in fantasies. We were pulling into the driveway after a light rain had just fallen. As I was parking, I looked up and noticed that there was a rainbow in the sky. I immediately got excited because I figured that Nyelle had never seen a rainbow, and this would be an awesome moment to share with my daughter. I parked the car, unclicked the car seat seatbelt, and excitedly pointed to the sky as a shouted, "Come Nye, look! There's a rainbow." She waddled over to where I was standing and took a 0.7 millisecond glance at the sky before declaring, "There's no rainbow." I was caught off guard by this and had to do a double take myself to verify that there indeed was a rainbow. After looking again and confirming that there was in fact a rainbow, I called her again and said, "Really Nye! Come! There's a rainbow!" She waddled back over to me and glanced at the sky and said, "Daddy you're silly. There's no rainbow."

Knowing that I surely was not senile at 29 years old, I asked myself why she couldn't see the rainbow that was in plain sight. Then it hit me. At this point in her life, the only rainbows that she had ever seen were in books, and videos. She has seen perfectly drawn, fantasy rainbows with clearly defined arches and colors. When she was directed to look at a real-life rainbow, she couldn't even acknowledge its beauty. She was so caught up in the perfection of a fantasy, that she was missing the beauty in her reality.

The Perfection of a Fantasy

One thing that is true about fantasies is that they are rarely ever imperfect. We must learn to navigate unrealistic expectations, meet students' needs effectively, and preserve the integrity of our work as educators amidst the challenges.

In today's education landscape, numerous teachers are leaving the profession due to unrealistic expectations imposed on them. Demands like achieving grade level mastery after the two-year hiatus of the pandemic or maintaining the same standards despite varying student circumstances can be overwhelming. Unfortunately, many educators receive insufficient empathy and support from districts, leading to feelings of inadequacy and discouragement.

To combat these pressures, we must acknowledge that unrealistic expectations exist but remain determined to provide our students with the best education possible. Ignoring external pressures and focusing on student growth is crucial. By nurturing their development and progress, we pave the way for eventual mastery, making the attainment of goals more organic and sustainable.

The journey to success is not without challenges, and it's essential to let go of the perfect of a fantasy. A fantasy says that we can reach all goals, meet each target, and rise to each expectation that is set by educational leaders. I understand why these goals, targets, and expectations are set, but I also understand that only in a perfect fantasy will they all be achieved. I would like to release you of the expectation to be perfect. If perfection is the goal, nobody ever scores.

When confronted with unrealistic expectations, remember that we possess unique gifts and talents that enable us to connect with our students. As educators, we are better equipped to assess their needs and cater our teaching accordingly. It is vital to stand firm and not allow mandates from outsiders to dictate how we teach. Our impact in the classroom is far-reaching, and we should harness our strengths to make a real difference in our students' lives.

Prioritizing growth over immediate mastery is the key to success. When we focus on nurturing students' progress, they are more likely to achieve mastery in due time. Sometimes, mandates and standards might not align with our students' developmental stages or diverse backgrounds. However, by prioritizing growth, we ensure that they progress steadily, building essential skills and knowledge along the way.

I have experienced firsthand how emphasizing growth leads to remarkable results. As mentioned before, I was school-level Teacher of the Year two times in two different states, and neither time was it because my students had the highest proficiency on the state exams. It couldn't be. Teacher of the Year is determined before those tests are even taken. Both times I was selected as Teacher of the Year it was because my students showed tremendous **growth** over the course of the year. I am a firm believer that when growth is prioritized, mastery is inevitable. Even if it doesn't happen immediately, it will happen eventually.

It's essential to set realistic and meaningful goals for our students, tracking their progress diligently. Growth is a powerful indicator of success, and when it becomes our priority, mastery will naturally follow. Growth generates belief in themselves, and once they believe, they can learn anything.

As educators, we must not be disheartened by unrealistic expectations imposed from external sources. Instead, we should focus on the reality that we have an opportunity to influence our students' growth, knowing that it is the driving force behind their long-term success. By embracing the beauty in our reality and nurturing each student's unique journey, we can provide the education they truly need and make a lasting impact on their lives.

The Fantasy of a Better Situation

We also sometimes get caught up in the fantasy that some other teacher has it easier or better, or that he or she hit the lottery of better, smarter, more engaged students. As the old saying goes, "the grass is always greener on the other side."

The saying refers to the perception that other people or situations seem better or more desirable than one's current circumstances and is often used to caution against envy, dissatisfaction, or the belief that one's own situation is inherently less favorable than others.

The origin of this saying can be traced back to ancient times. In fact, one of the earliest recorded instances is found in Roman poet Ovid's work "Heroides," written around 20 BCE, where he states, "The harvest is always richer in another man's field." It appeared in multiple literary works, such as the 1842 novel "The Tenant of Wildfell Hall" by Anne Brontë, where she wrote, "But we are all so prejudiced in our own favor that we are ever ready to make the worst interpretations."

The saying has endured over the years due to its relatability and timelessness. It resonates with human nature's tendency to compare ourselves to others and desire what we don't have, leading to the perception that other people's circumstances are more appealing than our own. Ultimately, the saying serves as a reminder to appreciate and value our own lives and experiences rather than constantly longing for what others may appear to have.

Embrace the Beauty of Your Reality

We get so captivated by the idealized perfection depicted in books, videos, and media that we can't appreciate the beauty in her own reality. We should not be fixated on idealized images of success but rather embrace what we have. The true value lies in the progress students make under our guidance, not merely in meeting arbitrary standards.

In our modern world, we are constantly bombarded with images of idealized perfection. From glossy magazines showcasing flawless models to carefully curated social media feeds displaying seemingly picture-perfect lives, we are constantly exposed to a world that appears to be without blemishes or imperfections. This influx of idealized images seeps into our subconscious, creating unrealistic expectations and leaving us yearning for something beyond our grasp.

In life, unexpected challenges and crises are inevitable. Sometimes, despite our best efforts and meticulous planning, things go wrong. It could be a sudden crisis, an unforeseen event, or a global pandemic like the one that forced schools to shut down for an extended period, disrupting the familiar rhythms of education.

In times of uncertainty, our ability to adapt, pivot, and accept the situation becomes paramount. Resilience and flexibility are essential qualities that help us navigate through these challenging times. As educators, it is crucial to acknowledge that setbacks are a part of the journey and that we must be prepared to face them head-on.

The pandemic was an unprecedented event that disrupted education worldwide. It compelled educators to quickly shift to remote learning, navigating uncharted territory and embracing digital tools to connect with students virtually. It was a test of our adaptability, and many teachers rose to the occasion, finding innovative ways to engage students and maintain a sense of community, even in a virtual setting.

In times of crisis, it is natural to feel overwhelmed and uncertain. However, accepting the reality of the situation is the first step towards finding solutions. Embracing the fact that challenges are a part of life helps us approach them with a growth mindset, viewing them as opportunities for learning and growth rather than insurmountable obstacles.

Moreover, acknowledging that things can go wrong allows us to be more compassionate with ourselves and others. It is essential to remember that everyone is facing their unique struggles and that it is okay to ask for help or seek support when needed. As educators, supporting each other and our students through difficult times fosters a sense of community and strengthens our collective resilience.

Adjusting and pivoting are essential skills, enabling us to respond effectively to changing circumstances. "Adjusting" is what propelled a once-failing entrepreneur to success. Fusajiro Yamauchi tried many business ventures including playing card manufacturer, vacuum cleaner company, instant rice distributor, and taxi service - named Nintendo. Though the early business ventures didn't last, he adjusted, and created one of the most profitable video game companies ever. "Pivoting" is what allowed Starbucks to change from selling espresso machines and coffee beans in 1971, to fresh brew coffee all over the world in the present day. As educators, we must be open to exploring new approaches and be willing to adapt our teaching strategies to meet the needs of our students.

Through it all, maintaining a positive and solution-oriented mindset is key. While we may not have control over external circumstances, we can control our attitude and response. Cultivating a mindset of acceptance and adaptability empowers us to face challenges with determination and find creative solutions.

In the realm of education, this phenomenon is not exempt. Teachers, too, can fall into the trap of being captivated by the illusion of perfection depicted in books, videos, and media. We may find ourselves comparing our classrooms to those showcased in carefully edited teaching tutorials or glamorous portrayals of educators in movies and TV shows. The pressure to emulate these portrayals can be overwhelming, causing us to lose sight of the true beauty and uniqueness of our own reality.

It is essential to recognize that perfection is an unattainable goal. True beauty lies not in achieving some idealized standard but in embracing and celebrating the diversity and progress of our students. Every student comes to us with their own set of strengths, challenges, and dreams. As educators, our responsibility is to provide a nurturing and supportive environment that allows each student to flourish in their own way.

When we shift our focus away from chasing perfection and instead embrace what we have, we can appreciate the beauty of every small victory and milestone in our students' journeys. It's not merely about meeting arbitrary standards or reaching predetermined benchmarks; it's about empowering our students to grow, learn, and develop at their own pace.

The reality is that sometimes beauty is ugly. What we attain in the end is beautiful, but the fight to get there can be brutal. This is true everywhere in life, so why not also in education. In the realm of art and aesthetics, there exists a genre known as "ugly beauty." Artists intentionally create works that challenge conventional notions of beauty, exploring the complexities and contradictions of human emotions and experiences.

Similarly, in nature, certain phenomena may be considered both beautiful and ominous. A thunderstorm, for instance, with its dramatic lightning, roaring thunder, and dark, brooding clouds, can be a breathtaking sight while simultaneously evoking feelings of unease and vulnerability. The power and grandeur of such natural occurrences remind us of the impermanence and uncontrollable forces that shape our world. And it is overwhelmingly beautiful.

On a deeper level, the concept of "ugly beauty" can be applied to the human experience. Often, we encounter situations that appear challenging, heartbreaking, or tragic, yet they carry a profound sense of beauty hidden within. Moments of struggle and adversity can lead to personal growth, resilience, and empathy. The beauty in these experiences lies in the strength and courage displayed in overcoming obstacles, the capacity for compassion, and the appreciation for life's inherent complexities.

Moreover, the concept of "ugly beauty" extends to the imperfections and vulnerabilities within ourselves and others. Our flaws, insecurities, and struggles contribute to our unique identity. Embracing our imperfections allows us to cultivate authenticity and empathy towards others, recognizing that everyone carries their own burdens and scars, making each individual beautiful.

By allowing for reality to be a bit challenging, we foster a culture of growth and development, where the emphasis is on progress rather than fixed outcomes. We celebrate each student's unique path and acknowledge that success is not a one-size-fits-all concept. Some students may make rapid strides in their learning journey, while others may require more time and support. Every step forward, no matter how small, is a cause for celebration and an affirmation of our impact as educators. It doesn't matter about the speed of their progression; all that matters is that they are moving in the right direction.

By embracing the beauty of our reality, we create a positive and nurturing learning environment where students feel valued and supported. As we let go of the pressure to meet unrealistic standards, we can focus on what truly matters: fostering a love of learning, building confidence, and nurturing a growth mindset in our students. We can stop focusing on the perfection of these fantasies and see the beauty in our realities.

Chapter 13: You Are Enough

"You are enough not because you did or said or thought or bought or became or created something special, but because you always were."

– Marisa Peer

Doubters will say that you can't make an impact because you alone are not enough. Ignore them.

I've said it several times throughout this book: "You are enough." Expect to hear it several more times before the end of this book because it is the central message of this book. There are so many ways in which teachers prove that they are enough. One of the most striking is what happened in 2020 when schools could no longer meet in person.

I remember being in the middle of an eighth-grade math lesson when I saw the notification from the principal telling us to send work home with students because we were closing for two weeks due to COVID-19. At the time I had no idea that it would be my last day ever in the classroom as a teacher.

The COVID-19 pandemic brought about an unprecedented disruption to education, challenging the traditional notion of classrooms. As schools closed their physical doors to curb the spread of the virus, educators and students were forced to adapt rapidly to remote learning, transforming our homes into makeshift classrooms.

In this time of crisis, kitchens, bedrooms, and dining room tables became the new learning spaces. Students logged into virtual classrooms, and teachers leveraged digital platforms to continue delivering lessons and engaging with our students. What seemed like an insurmountable task, transitioning to digital learning, was achieved in a matter of a month or two, defying the skepticism that it couldn't be done.

The swiftness with which educators embraced digital learning was a testament to our dedication, resilience, and adaptability. We quickly mastered new technologies, explored innovative teaching methods, and demonstrated remarkable creativity in reaching students. Despite the challenges of the digital divide, where not all students had equal access to devices and internet connectivity, educators found ways to bridge the gap to try to ensure that no student was overlooked.

Parents also became essential partners in this transformation, stepping into roles as co-teachers and offering support to their children during remote learning. The pandemic redefined the concept of education, breaking down barriers between school and home and fostering a deeper level of involvement from families in their children's learning journey.

While the shift to remote learning was monumental, it was not without its challenges. Educators grappled with the limitations of technology, the lack of face-to-face interaction, and the need to create a virtual classroom environment that was conducive to learning. However, we remained committed to providing their students with the best education possible, even in the face of adversity.

As we emerge from the pandemic, the lessons learned during this challenging period will undoubtedly shape the future of education. The experience has demonstrated that education can transcend physical boundaries, and that classrooms can exist beyond the walls of a school building. It has shown that, with determination and creativity, educators can overcome obstacles and adapt to ever-changing circumstances. But, most importantly, it showed that teachers are enough.

What may have seemed impossible before was achieved when driven by a shared purpose and a commitment to the well-being and education of students. It showed us that even in the most difficult of times, the human spirit can rise to the occasion, and through innovation and collaboration, we can transform adversity into opportunity.

If we could make such sweeping changes and still survive, I wonder what we could do in times of peace and tranquility. And now that we have widespread access to technology, it is time to push the boundaries even farther.

In the midst of the challenges posed by the pandemic, we educators found ourselves competing with a myriad of distractions like TikTok and Twitch, making student engagement even more elusive. Despite our best efforts, we occasionally question our impact and struggle with doubts about our abilities.

Let me share this powerful secret with you: You are enough. Your dedication, passion, and drive to improve students' lives are evident in your relentless pursuit of finding ways to help them succeed. Your commitment to researching, studying, and trying different methods shows that you genuinely care about your students and their growth.

It may seem like you're not reaching every student every day, and you might feel like you're drowning in uncertainty. However, remember that you are not alone in this uncharted territory. There was no handbook for navigating a pandemic-induced education landscape, but you did it. Whether you were teaching, in college, or even in high school still (Shoutout to Gen Z educators) you were part of the greatest educational revolution in a century that will forever shape the future of education. Your willingness to search for solutions and improve demonstrates that you are enough.

This doesn't mean you should stop searching or giving your best. The journey of learning and evolving as an educator never ends. But what I will say to you is,

Don't allow doubt to drown out your determination. Doubt can be a dream killer, but as long as your determination outweighs it, you will succeed.

Here's a tip to reinforce this belief in yourself: Practice self-affirmations regularly. Remind yourself how amazing you are, how capable, strong, and confident you are as an educator. Affirmations can build your confidence, erase doubt, and empower you to keep moving forward, finding ways to engage your students. If it is possible, you are capable.

Below are 20 teacher affirmations to help you get started:

For free bonuses and a printable poster of these affirmations, scan the code below or visit:

www.onepercentamazing.com/resources

20 Teacher Affirmations

— I am a passionate and dedicated educator, committed to making a positive impact on my students' lives.

— I believe in my ability to engage and inspire every student in my classroom.

— My enthusiasm for learning is contagious, and my students are eager to explore new ideas.

— I am adaptable and open-minded, embracing changes and challenges with confidence.

— I am a lifelong learner, continuously seeking new knowledge and professional growth.

— I create a safe and inclusive learning environment where all students feel valued and respected.

— I celebrate the uniqueness of each student, understanding that diversity enriches the classroom experience.

— I am patient and understanding, recognizing that each student learns at their own pace.

— I effectively communicate and connect with my students, building strong relationships based on trust and empathy.

— I am resilient and remain positive in the face of setbacks or difficulties.

— I encourage a growth mindset in my students, empowering them to embrace challenges and learn from mistakes.

— I foster a love for learning by making lessons engaging, relevant, and meaningful.

— I believe in the potential of every student, helping them unlock their talents and abilities.

— I am a supportive and encouraging mentor, guiding my students towards their goals and dreams.

— I am a creative problem solver, finding innovative solutions to overcome obstacles in the learning process.

— I prioritize student well-being, considering their social and emotional needs as well as academic growth.

— I collaborate effectively with colleagues and parents, creating a strong support network for my students.

— I am organized and prepared, ensuring that each lesson is structured and purposeful.

— I embrace a growth mindset for myself, continuously striving to improve as an educator.

— I am grateful for the opportunity to educate and shape the future, and I approach each day with enthusiasm and dedication.

Here's a pro tip. When you start saying an affirmation whether it's for weight loss, financial goals, or becoming a better teacher, your brain will initially reject and dismiss it. Affirmations become powerful as they are repeated. It may take saying it ten times followed by writing it ten times followed by recording yourself saying it ten times and playing that recording while you brush your teeth. Do whatever it takes to ensure you are overcoming imposter syndrome and the natural tendency to doubt. Once you get the affirmation embedded in your psyche, choose another one and then say them both. Keep adding more until you can say and believe them all. It doesn't matter which one you start with. Just start and the process of believing in your superb ability will be underway.

You possess the qualities of resilience, grit, and determination, just like I do. I, too, experience moments of doubt, but I refuse to let it define me. I believe in my ability to figure things out and reach students. And I believe the same for you. By reciting your affirmations regularly and wholeheartedly believing in yourself, you can transform your mindset and overcome any challenges that come your way.

Remember, you are a lifelong student as well, continually striving for excellence, and embracing the fact that excellence is not merely an exception but your expectation. So, keep pushing forward, keep engaging, and keep believing in your ability to make a difference in the lives of your students. You don't need more "stuff." You already have it. Dr. Suess was trying to win a bet when he wrote one of the best-selling children's books of all time. Bennett Cerf challenged that Dr. Seuss would not be able to write an entertaining children's book using only 50 different words. *Green Eggs and Ham*, was published in response to that challenge. He proved to us that it is less about your resources, and more about your resourcefulness. How can you maximize what you already have? All that you are, is all that you need. You are enough.

Chapter 14: Prioritize Tasks to Achieve More

"The idea of balance is a good one, when viewed with two Caveats:

1. Not everything in our lives deserves the same weight. Aim instead for the correct weight.

2. Balance isn't a daily act. Not everything will be given attention every day, and that's ok.

— Brooke McAlary, Slow: Simple Living for a Frantic World

Doubters will say that you can't make an impact because you have too many tasks to complete. Ignore them.

Let's start with a riddle. A plane is running out of fuel mid-flight and starts to take a nose-dive crash landing. The oxygen masks come down between you and your kids, what should you make sure happens first? Most people might say, "Put the oxygen mask on yourself first, then save my kids." But my response is, "Make sure there is enough fuel in the plane." Why would you board a flight without enough fuel to reach your destination?

Do you think I cheated with that riddle? I didn't. The top priority is making sure the plane has enough fuel to make it, so that you avoid a mid-air emergency. As educators, it is important for us to also identify our top priorities amongst the plethora of things we have to do. Once we step into the building, we are inundated with tasks back-to-back-to-back-to-back until that final bus pulls off at the end of the day and we can breathe. With so many tasks and responsibilities to attend to, we need to prioritize properly to avoid calamities and stay productive.

Becoming productive is a powerful discussion because it can multiply your effectiveness and impact. The role of a teacher involves juggling countless tasks, and it's easy to feel overwhelmed. To avoid this, many people have adopted some sort of framework to help them organize tasks. A popular framework is the Eisenhower Matrix. This matrix was made popular by President Dwight Eisenhower. He developed and used this matrix during his roles as US Army General, Supreme Allied Commander of NATO Forces, and President of the United States. It's safe to say he had almost as many critical decisions to make as educators.

I'll share with you my modified version of the Eisenhower Matrix, called the Impact-Based Matrix, to help you manage your time efficiently.

First, you might ask: Why use a matrix instead of a simple checklist? Well, a checklist often makes everything seem like a priority, and when everything is a priority, nothing is. When we have items on a list, there is no method to how we complete tasks. Sometimes we complete easy tasks first, or things with a close deadline first. The issue with this is that we find ourselves consistently running and jumping from task to task with no end in sight. In Chapter 4 we learned how to avoid burnout. This matrix ties in perfectly as through use of the Impact-Based Matrix, we can identify tasks based on their urgency and impact on our overall vision. The different quadrants help us to prioritize tasks.

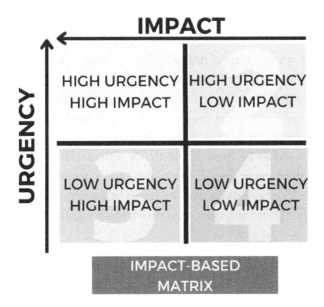

Let us first define "Urgency" and "Impact." "Urgency" relates to the deadline for a task to be completed. If there is not one given, create one. I personally adjust my matrix weekly. When I look at the matrix, all the tasks that need to be competed this week are in the top two quadrants as I consider those "high urgency." Tasks in the bottom two quadrants have deadlines that are further than a week out. You can adjust this to fit what works for you.

"Impact" is how the task relates to your overall vision. We created a vision in Chapter 2 that drives the work that you do. Every task that comes up has an impact on your vision. Some are very highly impactful, and some are not so impactful. The tasks that have a high impact on your vision should reside on the left side of the matrix.

With those terms defined, let's break down each quadrant. As I mentioned earlier, Quadrant One and Quadrant Two are at the top and are where we place the tasks with the highest urgency. Quadrant One contains tasks with a significant impact on our vision that need to be done immediately. Quadrant Two has a slightly lower impact but still requires attention very soon. To stay productive, we begin by completing tasks in Quadrant One first, then move to Quadrant Two.

As we move down to Quadrants Three and Four, tasks here have deadlines further out, but still need consideration. Quadrant Three contains tasks with high impact but can be addressed later. Quadrant Four includes less impactful tasks with a more distant deadline.

In the Eisenhower Matrix, it was suggested that we should be avoiding these tasks in Quadrant Four altogether. However, I believe in acknowledging all tasks and managing them effectively. So, if a task doesn't need to be done, it shouldn't be on our list in the first place.

This matrix helps you compare tasks to each other and your vision, making it easier to prioritize efficiently. As tasks are completed and added, adjust the matrix as needed based on changing deadlines or shifting priorities.

This matrix is a living document and will help you stay organized, avoid becoming overwhelmed, and focus on what truly matters. Remember, high impact tasks are aligned with your vision, so make sure you have a strong vision to guide your priorities effectively.

Productivity is not about doing more—it's about doing the right things at the right time. Embrace this system, and you'll discover newfound efficiency, success, and a sense of accomplishment. Try using the Impact-Based Matrix and take control of your time as a teacher. Avoid overwhelm and stay productive by putting the right tasks in the right places.

If you ever feel like you can't complete all the tasks in Quadrant One by the given deadline, don't worry. Reevaluate your definition of high impact and align it more closely with your vision. Sometimes we tend to view everything as the most important when somethings can move from Quadrant One to Quadrant Two.

You've got this! By using this matrix, you'll find yourself managing your tasks with confidence and achieving more than ever before. Stay organized, stay focused, and make this school year your most productive one yet!

For free bonuses and a digital version of this exercise, scan the code below or visit:

www.onepercentamazing.com/resources

Chapter 15: New Beginnings

"The chief beauty about time is that you cannot waste it in advance. The next year, the next day, and the next hour are lying ready for you, as perfect, as unspoiled, as if you had never wasted or misapplied a single moment in all your life. You can turn over a new leaf every hour if you choose."

— Arnold Bennett

Doubters will say that you can't make an impact because you got off to a bad start. Ignore them.

One of my favorite topics to cover is newness as a teacher whether that is the result of being a first-year teacher, transitioning to a new school, or just starting a new school year. It's also the topic about which I have a strong body of experience.

Transitioning to a new school year can be both exciting and overwhelming. I know because I've had five first days of school in new settings throughout my career, and I'll be honest, I made some mistakes during those transitions. However, with each experience, I learned valuable lessons.

Starting a new year, especially if it's your first year, a move to a new school, or a change in leadership, present unique obstacles that demand careful consideration. The key to making this a smooth transition lies in ten essential elements that will not only help you navigate the new terrain but also maximize your effectiveness in the classroom.

Tier 1: Getting Through the Tough Times

This tier is all about preventative system building. Think about it like car insurance. When my pregnant wife and toddler daughter were rear-ended on the way home from a playdate, the fact that insurance would cover car repairs and any hospital visits made the terrifying situation a little less stressful. When you move into a new school year, don't just accept issues and become stressed, rather anticipate issues and build systems.

1. Identify Your Support System: In the face of challenging moments, it's crucial to have a support network to lean on. Whether it's a family member, friend, or colleague, identify those who will help you navigate the tough times with their encouragement and understanding.

2. Develop Your Rebound Strategy: Tough times will undoubtedly arise, so it's essential to plan

your rebound strategy in advance. Determine activities or coping mechanisms that rejuvenate your spirit and help you bounce back with renewed energy.

3. Understand the Time Off and Sub Request Procedures: Life is unpredictable, and emergencies may occur. Familiarize yourself with the school's time-off and substitute request procedures early on to avoid unnecessary stress during critical situations.

Tier 2: Identify Your Supports Within the Building

This tier is all about humility and vulnerability. Not two of our favorite words, but two necessary characteristics for a successful start to the year. You won't know everything. No one does. But you can utilize the people in the building to help you gain a better understanding.

4. Interact With Staff Beyond Your Immediate Team: While building relationships within your teaching team is crucial, don't limit yourself to just that circle. Reach out to teachers from various subjects and grades, as well as support staff, such as custodians, secretaries, and cafeteria workers. These connections can offer invaluable support and insights throughout the school year.

5. Create a List of Your Needs: Once you're on campus, rather than sporadically asking for things you may need, take time to list all the essential items you might need throughout the year. Seek guidance from a reliable staff member to know whom to approach for each item on the list, streamlining the process and saving you time in the future.

6. Get Another Teacher's Amazon Wishlist: Request a teacher's Amazon wish list to get ideas about what to put on yours. This list will be a treasure trove of insight into the specific needs and preferences of your students, helping you align your supplies with their requirements.

7. Acknowledge That You Don't Know Everything: Humility is a valuable trait, especially in a new environment. Acknowledge that you have much to learn and be open to seeking advice and guidance from your colleagues. Embrace a growth mindset and be receptive to new perspectives.

Tier 3: Relationship Building

This tier is all about becoming a valued part of the school community. You want to be able to adopt the norms of the school community as well as build relationships with all stakeholders. An easy way to be rejected is to come in guns blazing and ready to disrupt everything. Rather, learn what systems are already in place, and align with community expectations. If you eventually see something that could be improved, suggestions are only easily accepted once you are an accepted member of the community.

8. Know the Staff Communication Norm: Find out how the school usually communicates among staff members, whether through email, GroupMe, or another platform. Understanding and adhering to this norm will streamline your interactions and ensure you're not missing any vital information.

9. Get Involved Beyond Your Classroom: To make a lasting impact and expand your horizons, seek opportunities to get involved outside of your classroom. Consider coaching a team, leading a club, joining committees, or contributing to other school initiatives.

10. Set Your Vision for the Year: Before the school year commences, take time to set your vision for the year. Define your goals, aspirations, and the impact you wish to make on your students. A clear vision will keep you focused and motivated, guiding your actions throughout the year. Share your vision.

By following these ten essential steps, you'll navigate the transition to your new school year with confidence and grace. Remember, embracing change is an opportunity for growth, and your commitment to excellence will undoubtedly leave a lasting impression on both your students and fellow educators. Step into the new chapter of your teaching journey with determination, resilience, and the vision to make a positive impact.

Bonus

New Beginnings: First Year Teachers

I have a special love for first year teachers. I remember what it was like to come into the profession with nervous excitement, and ready to change the world, only for the students to show up and put a screeching halt to my optimism like a bug hitting a car windshield. I know that my experience was not unique to me.

I recently had a consultation with a first-year teacher who is going through a challenging phase. She had a heart of gold and put in tremendous effort, showing up every day for her students. However, she felt like she was falling short of her own expectations. This feeling of not making enough impact or living up to her purpose can be overwhelming.

If you can relate to her experience, know that you're not alone. Many educators, especially first-year teachers, face similar struggles. It's crucial to support one another during such times.

For that reason, I want to dedicate the next few paragraphs to first-year teachers. I've compiled a list of five essential lessons that can set you up for success

Here are the things I wish someone told me coming out of college:

- Surround Yourself with Strong Supports: You aren't as strong as your dream; you are as strong as your team. Strong support personnel can carry you to success. I used the word "surround" very intentionally. Around 2,000 years ago, the story was told of a man who was paralyzed from birth. News got out that there was a man coming into town that could heal him from his paralysis. The paralyzed man was excited about the potential of healing, but there was no way he could carry himself to the Healer. Luckily, the man had four caring friends that carried him to where he needed to go. They did what was necessary to get him in front of the Healer, and sure enough, he was healed.

  As I read this story, I was impressed by the fact that even though he couldn't move himself, he had four friends that carried him where he needed to go. Since he was lying flat on a mat, I imagine that the four friends had to be very strategic with how they carried him. They probably had one at the head, one at the foot, and one on either side. They completely surrounded him. In those times when you can't carry yourself, for you to be taken where you need to go you also need a minimum of these four people to surround you.

o In front of you: Your Guide. Have a support person who has been where you are and is where you eventually want to be. This person can serve as a guide, letting you know what things to look out for based on their experience along the journey that you are just beginning.

o Your right side: Your Support. Tinku Razoria said, "Everyone should have that person that they can tell the truth to when asked, how are you?" You need that person who is right by your side in the trenches. They understand what you are going through because they are going through it too. This person will be there to hear you vent, protect your mental health, and make sure you are available to show up for students by taking care of you first. Find a good support person and find them early.

o Your left side: Your Protector. This is the person that protects your blindside, also known as your accountability partner. The person who reminds you that testing begins next week, or that there is a staff meeting after school. You need that person who is on top of it and won't let you slip below expectations.

- o Behind you: Your Encourager. It is imperative to remember that you will definitely have tough times. In those moments, you need someone behind you to catch you so that you don't fall. This is the person that will catch your tears, and let you know that everything will be ok. Identify who would be your partner for the eventual "trust fall" that you will experience as you begin your teaching career.

- Be Yourself: Trying to be someone you're not in the classroom can be counterproductive. You will always have to be the fake version you presented to your coworkers. Instead, embrace your authentic self and let your true personality shine. Students appreciate genuineness, and they will respect and connect with the real version of you.

- Clear Expectations: Establishing clear expectations and consistent consequences is essential. Be fair and impartial when addressing students' behavior, ensuring that consequences are linked to *their* actions and not influenced by your emotions. As the old saying goes, "Well begun is half done." Start off by making sure students know your expectations. And always keep your promises. We'll learn more about classroom management in Chapter 21.

- Start Thinking About Retirement: Though it may seem far off, planning for retirement early in your career can make a substantial difference in the long run. Consult a financial advisor to understand the best strategies to save and invest for your future. You don't have to be a math teacher to understand this simple fact: The more time you spend saving towards retirement, the more you will have when you retire. The sooner you begin, the greater your potential to earn.

- Outside the Classroom: Engage with students outside of formal classroom settings by participating in clubs, coaching teams, or organizing virtual meetups. Building relationships beyond academic boundaries can lead to deeper connections and understanding. Be there. Let them see your face.

- Character & Life Skills: While content mastery is important, focusing on building students' character, life skills, and mindsets is equally vital. Encourage grit, resilience, and growth mindset to help students believe in their potential and succeed in all aspects of life.

As a first-year teacher, you may encounter challenges, but remember that every obstacle is an opportunity for growth. Keep learning, seeking improvement, and embracing the journey of teaching. Excellence is not an exception but an expectation, and there is greatness within you waiting to be unleashed. Stay committed to your purpose, and you will make a lasting impact on your students' lives.

SECTION 4

Improve Your Data

The following strategies are targeted at impacting middle school students. I am leading with that transparency because I don't want those who don't teach in middle school to become frustrated if the strategies as written don't positively impact their students. I intentionally chose to focus on a single grade span. I think about it like throwing darts. You have a better chance of hitting the bullseye if you precisely throw single darts one at a time, than you do if you hurl a handful of darts at the board at once hoping one hits. I don't want to give general information that may or may not work for your grade level, I want to present specific information to make a specific impact. Now your job, for those of you not teaching middle school, is to understand the principles being taught and adjust the specifics to meet the needs of your students. It is possible, and you are capable.

One of my best friends said something that I will never forget and that I believe is fully applicable in this upcoming section. My three closest friends, Brandon, Dominic, Morel, and I have a group video call every few weeks. We spend hours catching up, cracking up at college memories, and supporting each other through the new adventures in our lives. One Friday night, after 1am, while we were reminiscing on things we've experienced, Dominic said something that made us all pause. He said, "I don't regret anything I've ever done; my only regrets are from the things that I didn't."

What he meant by that was, even the decisions he made that didn't end up turning out like he anticipated, he is grateful that he took action because he was able to learn from the experience. The reason why I share that with you at the start of this section is because there is no guarantee that these eight strategies, as written, will have the same immense impact on your students as they did for me. But I can guarantee that if you don't try them, you'll never know. I need you to be brave enough to give them a try and know that you are smart enough to make the necessary adjustments to make it work for you and your students. No regrets. You've got this.

For student resources to complement the strategies in this section, check out the Choices Curriculum by visiting:

www.onepercentamazing.com/resources

Chapter 16: Motivate Unmotivated Students

"We never know which lives we influence, or when, or why."

— Stephen King

Indeed, teachers face numerous challenges and difficulties in their profession. Here's a list of some common complaints voiced by teachers. If you resonate with any of these, just blink three times, no one will notice.

- Heavy Workload: Teachers often find themselves overwhelmed with the sheer volume of lesson planning, grading, and administrative tasks, leaving little time for personal life or self-care.

- Lack of Resources: Many educators struggle with limited budgets and inadequate classroom resources, making it challenging to provide the best learning experiences for their students.

- Large Class Sizes: Managing a large class can be exhausting, as it becomes challenging to give individualized attention and address the diverse needs of every student.

- Lack of Support: Teachers may feel unsupported by administrators or parents, leading to feelings of isolation and frustration.

- Behavior Management Issues: Dealing with disruptive behavior and maintaining discipline in the classroom can be mentally and emotionally draining.

- Standardized Testing Pressure: Teachers often feel pressured to focus on test preparation, taking away from a more holistic approach to education.

- Inadequate Professional Development: Some educators feel that the professional development opportunities provided to them are not relevant or sufficient to address their specific needs.

- Time Constraints: Limited time for collaboration with colleagues or for planning creative and engaging lessons can hinder the teaching experience.

- Demands of Paperwork: Teachers must contend with administrative paperwork, which can take time away from instruction and personal development.

- Lack of Parent Involvement: A lack of parent engagement can hinder the educational progress of students and create communication challenges between teachers and parents.

- Salary and Benefits: Many teachers feel undervalued in terms of compensation and benefits, leading to dissatisfaction and attrition.

- Burnout: The cumulative effect of the above challenges can lead to burnout, causing some teachers to leave the profession.

Despite these challenges, dedicated educators persevere for one reason: their desire to make a positive impact on their students' lives. It's all that matters to most of us.

That's why it is more frustrating than failed contract negotiations when a student doesn't perform well. It breaks our hearts, shatters our confidence, and puts the spotlight on our classrooms.

To help students reach their full potential in your class, it's essential for them to understand why it matters. When we give them a reason to care, we give them a reason to show up.

When it comes to student motivation, there are three types of students.

Group one is already motivated and sees the purpose of your class and its content. These students already have a strong sense of purpose. They come to you with intrinsic drive, enthusiasm, and a clear dream.

Group two needs to be convinced of the purpose, as they don't immediately grasp its relevance. These students may express doubts about the relevance of the subject matter to their future goals. They question why they should pay attention in science class when they aspire to become a wig influencer, earning a living off brand deals, sponsorships, and affiliate marketing. As a teacher, it can be disheartening to hear such sentiments, especially when you know the importance of your content. However, it's crucial to empathize with these students and recognize that not all students will immediately see the connection between your class and their dreams. We'll uncover how to motivate this group in a moment.

Group three, on the other hand, lacks a clear dream and doesn't see the need for a purpose at all. They haven't developed a vision for their future. Therefore, these students lack motivation because they have no sense of direction. They might respond with indifference when asked about their career aspirations, often shrugging, or offering vague answers. These students are the embodiment of the famous Marshawn Lynch quote, "I'm just here so I won't get fined."

The goal in motivating students is to eradicate groups two and three in your classroom and bring all students into group one. That means that each student will have a dream and see how your particular class can help them achieve it. It is possible, and here is how.

Target group three first. Remember, these are the students that don't have a dream at all. The simple fix here, is to help them identify a dream. It is essential to recognize that not every student follows a linear path or has a clear sense of direction from the beginning. Many young minds go through their academic years without a specific vision of what they want to achieve or where they want to go. They find themselves merely going through the motions, attending school because it is expected of them.

As educators, we have the incredible opportunity to help them shape a dream they may not have yet realized. We can play a crucial role in nurturing their aspirations, helping them uncover their true passion and purpose. Creating a dream for our students goes beyond merely imparting knowledge; it involves fostering a sense of direction and self-awareness.

To create a dream for our students, we must engage them in meaningful exercises that encourage self-discovery and exploration. By asking thought-provoking questions and actively listening to their responses, we can help them identify their interests, strengths, and areas of genuine curiosity. For those who lack a vision and dream, it's crucial to help them create one.

A popular exercise to help people find their purpose is through the Ikigai Venn Diagram. "Ikigai" is a Japanese concept combing the terms "iki," meaning "life," and gai meaning "worth." This exercise helps people find "that which gives your life worth." I have modified it for students in the Venn Diagram below. Start by asking these four questions:

1. What are you good at doing?
2. What do you love to do?
3. What does the world need more of?
4. What can you be paid to do?

Allow students to list as many possible responses to those questions as they can think of. Then, using the Venn Diagram, place responses that appear in multiple categories in the appropriate segments. The goal is to find at least one response that appears in all four categories. That is a good choice to serve as that student's dream. That is Ikigai.

For free bonuses and a digital version of this exercise, scan the code below or visit:

www.onepercentamazing.com/resources

Our role as educators is not just to disseminate information but to be facilitators of growth and self-awareness. By guiding students through introspection and discussions, we can help them connect the dots between their abilities and their potential dreams. We can inspire them to envision a future where their passions align with their chosen paths.

In the process of creating a dream, we instill a sense of belief and confidence in our students. Many young minds may be hesitant to dream big due to self-doubt or fear of failure. We must reassure them that dreams can be nurtured and achieved with hard work, perseverance, and resilience. We might even be willing to go the extra mile and commit to helping them on their chosen path and offer advice from our own mishaps and success stories.

By sharing our own journeys and struggles, we can provide valuable insights and examples of how dreams can become reality through determination and dedication. Our stories can serve as a source of

Improve Your Data| 168

inspiration, showing students that even the most uncertain paths can lead to fulfilling and purposeful destinations.

Moreover, we can expose our students to diverse opportunities and experiences that broaden their horizons and expand their vision. Guest speakers, field trips, and community involvement can offer valuable insights and ignite passions they never knew they had.

In the process of creating a dream for our students, we must also be mindful of individual differences and tailor our approaches accordingly. Not all dreams are grand or dramatic; some may start as modest aspirations that grow into something extraordinary over time. Often parents and others in a child's life decide what the child's dream should be. Be careful not to do the same thing. Let the child guide the conversation with you there to ask the right questions to elicit honest responses. Even if you don't agree with the dream, allow them to chase it. As long as the dream is moral and ethical, let them have it.

"But Mr. Williams, what if half of my students say that want to be in the NBA?"

Let them dream! If they have gone through the Ikigai exercise and can <u>prove</u> to you that it firmly fits in all four sections (even "What does the world need more of?"), then let them dream. As long as they have future dreams and aspirations, you can use that to fuel their struggle. Dreams are the catalyst to motivation. Encourage the dream and hold them to high expectations to turn it into a reality. Besides, if any of them actually do achieve that dream, I'm sure that on opening night of the 2029-2030 NBA season, you'll be broadcasting, "I taught him!"

As educators, we are not simply molding minds; we are nurturing dreams. By taking the time to understand and engage with our students on a personal level, we can uncover their hidden potential and empower them to pursue their passions.

Creating a dream for our students is not a one-time event but an ongoing process. Continue to support and encourage them as they explore their interests and face the challenges that come their way. By fostering a culture of dream-chasing and self-discovery, we can shape the next generation of purpose-driven, motivated individuals ready to make a positive impact on the world.

By discovering their strengths, interests, and aspirations, you can help them form a compelling dream that provides a sense of purpose. And once students in group three have a dream, they are no longer in group three. Rather, they move into group two, and group three is eradicated.

Now that students are in group two, they have a dream, but might not be able to connect it to why your class is relevant. That's fine, there's a simple solution for that as well. In order to move students from group two to group one, you need to connect your class to their dream. Sometimes there is a clear link. Someone who wants to be a Chemist, should probably pay attention in Chemistry class. But sometimes the link is not as clear. In these situations, the first step is to acknowledge that the subject matter may not directly align with their dreams. Stick with me, I'm going somewhere.

You can emphasize that the learning experience itself is invaluable. Highlight the transferable skills, such as problem-solving, perseverance, and resilience, that they can develop while studying seemingly unrelated topics. Emphasize that overcoming challenges, learning new things, and developing important life skills are essential for success in any career.

For a period of time, I found myself unsure of my true calling, unsure of the path I should pursue. I had dreams but couldn't see why memorizing elements on the periodic table, or differentiating between a simile and a metaphor were relevant, unless I wanted to star on Jeopardy someday. My journey to discovering my passion led me to explore various fields, ranging from the medical domain to education, social work, and even theology. It seemed like I was scattered, exploring different avenues in search of the perfect fit, and that is okay, because I kept learning. I learned how to take unfamiliar topics and grapple with them until I understood them. I developed critical thinking skills when faced with problems that didn't have a clear solution. I grew in resilience when failing to achieve my goal but refusing to settle. I used my dreams as motivation to acquire more skills, and later in life those skills granted me choices. I was able to take advantage of the many choices I had, and follow my current dreams, because of the skills I acquired in classes I thought didn't matter.

Help students see the link between your class and their dream by teaching them that the in the gap between where they are and where they want to be, is the acquisition of skills that they don't yet have. And in your class, you are allowing them to build skills now, so that they can have choices later. Once students can see that, they are no longer in group two, but they are in group one, and group two is eradicated.

If you would like a "done-for-you" curriculum that teaches students which skills to build now so that they have choices later, visit:

www.onepercentamazing.com/resources

Let's recap. Students fall into one of three groups as it pertains to their motivation levels. Group One can align your content to their dreams and are therefore motivated. Group Two can't see how your content aligns to their dreams and are therefore less motivated. Group Three students do not have a dream at all and are therefore unmotivated. Ultimately, your goal is to move all students into Group One, where they are intrinsically motivated and see the value in your class.

Do this by giving the students in Group Three a dream. Once they all have dreams, they join Group Two, and Group Three no longer exists. With students who are in Group Two, align their dream to your content by highlighting transferrable skills. Once that link is created, Group Two is eradicated, and all students are in Group One.

Once all students are motivated, the way you keep them in Group One is by incorporating goal setting into your teaching methodology. Implement the SMARTER goal framework, where students set Specific, Measurable, Achievable, Relevant, Time-bound, Evaluated, and Rewarded goals. Encourage them to create goals that align with their dreams, thus maintaining the link between their aspirations and your class content.

Bonus – Dream Boards

Creating a dream board, also known as a vision board, is a powerful tool to help kids visualize and manifest their goals and dreams. This is an excellent activity for students who are in group three, or newly transitioned to groups one or two. It involves collecting images, words, and symbols that represent your aspirations and displaying them on a board or poster. Here's how and why to make a dream board:

1. Introduction:

Start by introducing the concept of dream boards to the students. Explain that a dream board is a visual representation of their goals and dreams, which can help them stay motivated and focused on achieving their aspirations. You might even (if you are comfortable with it) share your dream board with your students so that they will lower their defenses.

2. Ikigai:

Guide the students through the Ikigai exercise. Encourage them to think about what they want their gifts to be able to allow them to do. This allows students to not focus on a specific vehicle, but on where that vehicle can take them.

3. Collect Materials:

Provide students with magazines, newspapers, printed images, markers, colored pencils, scissors, glue, and poster boards. Ask them to bring in any materials they want to include on their dream boards.

4. Visualize Dreams:

Have the students flip through the magazines or use online resources to find images and words that represent their goals and dreams. Encourage them to choose items that evoke positive emotions and inspire them. Let them use technology by going online to find images or by creating a digital dream board to go along with their physical one.

5. Organize and Create:

Ask the students to arrange the selected images and words on their poster boards. They can create a collage-style layout or organize the materials by categories.

6. Add Personal Touches:

Encourage students to add their own drawings, artwork, or any other personal touches to make their dream boards unique and meaningful to them.

7. Share and Discuss:

After everyone has completed their dream boards, give each student the opportunity to share their boards with the class. This can be a great way for them to articulate their dreams and aspirations and learn from their peers. But don't force anyone. Give them agency and the right to keep their dreams private.

8. Display the Dream Boards:

Give the students the option to display their dream boards in the classroom or a designated area of the school where they can see them regularly. Having their dream boards in a prominent place will serve as a constant reminder of their goals. Again, some students may choose not to share and may want to post their dream board at home.

9. Review and Revisit:

Encourage students to regularly review and revisit their dream boards. Remind them that the dream board is a tool to keep them focused and motivated on their goals, and taking consistent action is crucial in achieving them.

10. Celebrate Achievements:

Celebrate and acknowledge any progress or achievements the students make towards their goals. This positive reinforcement can boost their confidence and determination.

11. Reflect and Revise:

Periodically allow students to reflect on their dream boards and revise them as their goals evolve or change. This helps them stay flexible and adapt to new aspirations.

12. Share with Me!

I would love to see how creative you get with this exercise. Take pictures and use the hashtag #onepercentamazing when posting to social media. I can't wait to see what you come up with!

Teaching students to create dream boards not only fosters their creativity but also encourages them to think critically about their goals and the steps needed to achieve them. It empowers them to take ownership of their dreams and work towards making them a reality.

Remember that a dream board is a tool, and while it can be highly motivating, it requires effort and action on your part to turn your dreams into reality. Regularly review your board, set smaller milestones, and take steps towards your goals to maximize its effectiveness. Stay persistent, and your dream board can be a valuable asset on your journey to success and fulfillment.

While motivating unmotivated students might seem like an arduous task, your efforts can have a profound impact on their academic growth and personal development. By recognizing their individual needs, helping them discover their dreams, and fostering a culture of goal setting and self-discovery, you can empower your students to reach their full potential in your class and beyond.

In the next chapter, we are going to detail the SMARTER Goal framework to keep students motivated and progressing towards success.

Chapter 17: Actually Achieve Classroom Goals

A dream written down with a date becomes a goal. A goal broken down into steps becomes a plan. A plan backed by action makes your dreams come true. - Greg S. Reid

SMARTER goals can lead to achieving significant student growth in your classroom and help you develop effective plans, ultimately resulting in improved student growth. As we move forward, you'll notice that current education faces challenges, such as teaching to the middle, neglecting advanced students, and ignoring struggling learners. However, post-pandemic education demands innovation. SMARTER goals represent that innovation.

In 2019, while teaching eighth-grade math, I successfully exceeded expected growth. Moreover, during the school year, I implemented the strategies I've shared in this book in two other schools, achieving outstanding results, like 114% growth in reading and transforming over half of the class to grade level.

The success of goal setting lies in two key factors. First, students are willing to face challenges when they care deeply about what they're striving for. Just like athletes endure rigorous training to win competitions, students will put in effort when they care about their academic goals. Secondly, students, just like everyone else, won't leave their current state until they envision where they want to be. My wife Shakira and I owned a basic Queen-sized mattress for the first several years of our marriage. On one vacation to Aruba, we slept on a state-of-the-art premium King-sized mattress that allowed us to have the best sleep we'd ever experienced. Shortly after we got back to the states, our very own premium King-sized mattress was purchased and delivered. One we saw where we'd rather be, we could no longer stay where we were. In the classroom, goal setting provides that vision and motivates students to take action to achieve it.

Setting SMARTER goals addresses those two key factors, as well as helps to create an accountability system so that goals are achieved. You may already be familiar with SMART goals, but the Evaluation and Reward phases (E and R in SMARTER) are what makes this framework more effective than any other that I have tried. First, let's cover SMART goals: Specific, Measurable, Achievable, Relevant, and Time-bound.

SMART

In education, SMART goals are an effective way to guide and measure students' progress and teachers' professional development. Let's break down how SMART goals can be applied in education:

Specific

Goals should be clear and well-defined. Instead of setting a broad goal like "Improve reading skills," make it more specific, such as "Increase reading fluency by twenty words per minute." Broad goals are ineffective because the brain needs actionable steps to make progress.

Measurable

Goals should be quantifiable, allowing you to track progress and determine if the objective has been achieved. For instance, you could measure progress by using reading assessments and comparing the student's fluency rate over time. Measurable goals are best because it's easy for kids to see their progress.

Achievable

Goals should be realistic and attainable. Set targets that are challenging yet within reach based on the student's abilities, resources, and time available for learning. I always like to ask students, "based on previous performance data, how do you know this goal is a fingertip goal?" A "fingertip goal" is one that is just within reach when you stretch as far as you can. We want fingertip goals, not depths of the ocean goals.

Relevant

Goals should align with the overall dream. Imagine that the dream is the top rung of a ladder. Every goal is a rung that gets you one step closer to the top. If your dream is for every student to realize their full potential, a goal of 90% mastery on the End of Grade assessment is not relevant in your class. All students can grow and the class still not be at 90%. That means the dream can be realized without this goal being achieved, making it irrelevant. In this case, perhaps try setting a goal of everyone reaching their individualized growth goals by the end of the year.

Time-bound

Goals should have a specific timeline for completion. Set a deadline for achieving the goal, which creates a sense of urgency and helps monitor progress effectively. For example, "Increase reading fluency by twenty words per minute within the next three months."

"SMART Goals" is probably the most common type of goal setting approach in schools. The acronym is clean, memorable, and relevant. However, when I was reading "Atomic Habits" by James Clear, the author made a point that will stick with me forever. He pointed out the fact that anyone can *set* goals. Both successful people and unsuccessful people set goals. So that means that the *setting* of goals cannot be the sole indicator of whether or not someone will be successful.

What determines the success of the goal are the actions taken after the goal is set. The real strength in the goal achievement process is not found in goal *setting*, it is in goal *chasing*. Those who are successful do not rise to the height of the goal, they rest on the strength of their systems. And when we look at SMART Goals, the area that is unaddressed is, "What happens after the goals are set?" That's where the **SMARTER** Goals framework steps in to help you achieve the goals you set. The following two components are game changers.

Evaluated

The first component that converts goal *setting* into goal *chasing* is the evaluation of progress along the way. The best way I can describe the evaluation process, is by marveling at my Dad's amazing channel flipping skills.

If you grew up anything like me in the early 2000's, you are probably familiar with the concept of channel flipping. In my household, channel flipping took place on Monday nights when my Mom, Dad, three younger siblings, and occasionally a few cousins, would pile into the living room after dinner and huddle around the one big screen box TV in the house. This was the place to be because this was the TV with the cable box. That meant that we could all tune in live to watch our favorite new hit reality TV show, "American Idol." I can remember watching the auditions, and the elimination rounds, and all of us singing along the best we could as if Simon, Paula, and Randy were going to give us feedback. But the thing that stands out to me the most is how Ryan Seacrest would kick to commercial, and what would happen next. "Who will make it to the next round? You'll find out…after the break." As we all sat on the edge of the couch in anticipation, suddenly the TV would flash, and we'd see the New York Knicks losing to some other NBA team. My Dad had "channel flipped."

I don't know if it was because he couldn't stand commercials, or he didn't want to miss the game, but his channel flip was swift. Here's what I want to note about his process. Every thirty seconds or so, he would flip back to channel five to check and see if American Idol had come back on. If it was not on, back to channel twenty-four we went, to watch the game. The family would get nervous every time he flipped back to the game because we feared we would miss the big reveal! But he was unbothered and stuck with his process. Eventually after a few cycles of channel flipping, he would flip back to channel five and with pristine timing he would land back on Fox just as Ryan Seacrest announced, "America has voted. Your American Idol is…Kelly Clarkson!"

I used to think his channel flipping timing accuracy was some sort of superpower. But I now understand that the perfect precision was the product of a practiced process. He flipped to channel five every thirty seconds or so to gauge how long it would be until the show returned. The way he was able to get back just in time, was by consistently checking in along the way. I would like to argue that if he hadn't created a check-in process, and just tried to flip back once, right when the show was starting again, his accuracy would have been a lot lower percentage. It is the same process with goal chasing. Too many people set a goal, assign a time, and hope for the best. They don't review their progress, they just come back when time is up and see how they did. That may work with clothes in the washer machine, but not classroom goals.

In order to achieve the goals that you set in the classroom, it is imperative to evaluate the progress along the way. When you do that, you can make adjustments to make sure that you stay on track to reach the goal. Whatever the timeline is, create a consistent and reasonable cadence where you intentionally pause to discuss the progress. A great idea is to set individual student conferences. I used to do them on the day after a test, when students were working on test corrections. I would pull each student to my desk individually and have a brief sixty second or less check-in. I would remind them of the goal, show them where they are, and tell them what they need to do. It was at this juncture that I would help students to recognize that they either had to adjust their **grind** or adjust their **goal**.

Adjusting their grind is pretty straightforward. If they were capable of doing more to achieve that goal, I would remind them that they were, and encourage them to increase their effort (giving practical tips of course). But if during check-in we realized that the goal was incorrectly set, we can adjust the goal. Some people get confused by that, so let me explain.

When we set the goal, we made sure it was relevant based on previous performance data. But it is possible that the goal was still not a fingertip goal. Perhaps the goal is too easy. Maybe the goal was for students to achieve a year's worth of growth by the end of the year, and after a quarter they are 80% of the way there. We can adjust that goal. Change it from a year's worth to 1.5 years' worth. Show them that you recognize their abilities so much so that you won't insult them by giving them a goal that's so easy to hit.

But there is also the option that the goal that you set was too lofty. That happens. And rather than leave a goal that is incredibly unrealistic to hit, which can hurt student confidence and morale, adjust the goal down to one that is within reach. I like to think about it like the end of a blowout game in professional sports. The team starts with a goal to win. Great goal. Somewhere down the line during the game, things got away from them. Now there are three minutes left and they're down by forty. In most cases, they put in the backups, and hope to just finish the game. The goal changed. They realized that the initial goal, winning, was now incredibly unrealistic, and rather than risking hurting their players, they changed the goal to just finishing, and they go back to practice the next day to regroup. It is okay to change the goal when you realize that keeping it will do more harm than good.

Be intentional about the check-in process and make the necessary adjustments along the way. My suggestion is to put the evaluation dates on the calendar at the same time that the goal is set.

If you would like a digital template of the evaluation calendar that I used, visit:

www.onepercentamazing.com/resources

Reflected/Rewarded

What leads to continued success as it pertains to goal chasing and achieving, is reflecting on the success or failure of a goal. When chasing goals, sometimes you win, sometimes you lose, but every time you must learn. When you win, reflect on what went well that led to that success. When you lose, reflect on what caused the class to fall short. It is when we reflect over the system and outcome that we can create continued success.

It is common for people to reflect when they lose, but reflecting after a win is less common. What I am about to say might be the most important sentence of this chapter. Success is not an accident, and failure is not definite. One does not accidentally stumble into success. It is the result of smart systems, and strong effort. When the process is reflected on and repeated, the repeated success is eminent. And when failure happens, as it definitely will, it is not the end of the story. When shortcomings are reflected on and improved upon, it is hard to repeat the same failure. Instead, growth towards success is what ensues. Therefore, failure isn't really failure at all. It is just delayed success.

When success is achieved, a reward is a great way to celebrate. Yes, it is true that the intrinsic value of achieving a goal is great, but it is also true that an extrinsic reward is a great motivator. Extrinsic rewards can give someone the extra dopamine push to give maximum effort. People who are opposed to incentivizing with an extrinsic reward are afraid that the students will just "do it for the prize" and have no actual intrinsic desire to be great. That simply is not true. Intrinsic desire and extrinsic motivation can both co-exist. Think about it. NFL players don't go through years of literal physical torture just for the ability to hold a twenty-two-inch trophy. But when you see them on Superbowl Sunday with confetti falling from the sky, they hoist that trophy with tears in their eyes. You didn't go through years of annoying roommates, unrealistic professors, and all-night study session just to hold a blank 8.5" x 11" paper with a ribbon around it. But I guarantee you smiled big while holding it in the photo. It is not the Superbowl Trophy or the diploma that serves as the sole purpose of why we choose to struggle while goal chasing, but the fact that they exist give a little extra motivation. The same is true for students in your class.

When deciding on the goal, also decide on the reward. In Chapter 23 we will talk about what rewards to use, and how to utilize those rewards, but for now, just know that they need to exist and students need to know what it will be.

For a digital template of this goal setting framework, visit:

www.onepercentamazing.com/resources

Now that you know how to set and chase goals, we have to make sure that students believe that they can achieve them. It is not enough for you to tell them how great they are, they also have to tell themselves. In the next chapter, we will uncover how to utilize positive student affirmations.

Chapter 18: Positive Student Affirmations

"You spend most of your life inside your head. Make it a nice place to be."

- Unknown

To empower our students and foster their self-belief, we should practice daily affirmations. We can recognize their capabilities and aim to instill the confidence they need to succeed. Our intention should be to encourage them to believe in themselves, just as we do.

Training students to believe in themselves is crucial for their personal development, well-being, and future success. The National Center for Education Statistics has reported the following as it pertains the power of positive student affirmations:

"Brain scans have confirmed that the use of positive self-affirmations triggers a corresponding release of chemicals in the brain that can be used to acquire new information,

> thus leading to increased
> academic performance and
> closing of the achievement gap."

This substantiates something I always say about students who are self-empowered and are willing, which is, "I can turn willingness into mastery." When students use self-affirmations to increase their motivation, we can take it from there. There are several reasons why fostering self-belief is important. Obviously, the first and most important reason is that they do better in school, get better grades, are more likely to further their education, and grow into lifelong learners. But there's so much more students gain than good grades.

- Positive Self-Image: Believing in oneself cultivates a positive self-image. When students have confidence in their abilities and value their uniqueness, they are more likely to have a strong sense of self-worth and self-acceptance.

- Resilience: Self-belief contributes to resilience. Students who believe in themselves are better equipped to handle setbacks and challenges. They view failures as learning opportunities and are more likely to bounce back from adversity.

- Motivation and Effort: Students with self-belief are motivated to put in effort and strive for excellence. When they believe they can achieve their goals, they are more likely to work hard and persevere, leading to improved academic and personal achievements.

• Growth Mindset: As we've already discussed, a growth mindset is more useful than a fixed mindset. Believing in oneself is closely tied to developing a growth mindset. Students with a growth mindset understand that their abilities and intelligence can be developed through effort and learning. This mindset encourages them to embrace challenges and continuously improve.

• Risk-taking: Self-belief empowers students to take calculated risks. When they believe in their capacity to handle new experiences and challenges, they are more likely to step out of their comfort zones, explore new opportunities, and embrace innovation.

• Emotional Well-being: Believing in oneself contributes to emotional well-being. It reduces feelings of self-doubt, anxiety, and stress. Students who have self-confidence are more likely to experience greater emotional resilience and overall mental health.

• Interpersonal Relationships: Self-belief influences how students interact with others. When they believe in themselves, they are more likely to engage in healthy relationships, assert their opinions, and contribute positively to group dynamics.

• Aspirations and Goals: Students with self-belief are more likely to set ambitious goals and aspirations for their future. They have the confidence to pursue their dreams, whether in academics, careers, or personal passions.

• Leadership and Advocacy: Self-belief prepares students for leadership roles. When they have confidence in their abilities, they are more likely to step up, take initiative, and advocate for themselves and others.

• Life Satisfaction: Ultimately, self-belief contributes to overall life satisfaction. Students who believe in themselves tend to lead more fulfilling lives, as they are empowered to pursue their passions, achieve their goals, and contribute positively to their communities.

Fostering self-belief in students equips them with a strong foundation for personal growth, resilience, and success. By instilling confidence and a positive mindset, educators empower students to navigate life's challenges and opportunities with a sense of purpose and determination.

Teaching students to use affirmations can be a powerful way to help them develop a positive growth mindset, boost their self-confidence, and enhance their overall well-being. Of course, crafting affirmations demands personalization. The overarching principle remains consistent: daily affirmations nurture self-assuredness. By tailoring these affirmations to our students' specific needs, we prepare for a lifetime of positivity about themselves and their education.

I remember my first-year teaching when I was trying to find myself, like all first-year teachers do. I was struggling with my classroom management so much, that my principal at the time admitted to struggling to renew my contract for year two. It was not a safe environment for children and could become a liability to the school. Over the course of the year, I did have co-workers that tried to help. I can remember one co-worker in particular that also taught math. Her class was always pin-drop silent. It was the polar opposite of mine. When you walked past her classroom, students didn't even glance up and look towards the door as many students do. Meanwhile, in my class, at any given moment if you looked towards my room from down the hall, you could see students in and out of my doorway like a NYC subway turnstile. She noticed this about my management and offered some advice:

"You just gotta Hulk up on 'em Williams. You too soft wit 'em. Let them see that Hulk come out."

I received the feedback, and went back to my room, in search of my inner Hulk. See, my co-worker was a former D1 college basketball center. She stood over six feet tall and weighed somewhere around the 250lb mark. She had booming voice, and a stern look. Me on the other hand, I was a 5'7" former High School long-distance runner with a calm demeanor and chill personality. I searched deep for The Hulk within, but I never found him.

What I did find, was how to utilize my natural gifts, talents, and abilities to manage my class effectively and on my terms. That is what allowed me to transition from a terrible teacher to a two-time teacher of the year. We will uncover the systems that I found to be effective in Chapters 21 and 22, but for now just know that my students didn't need The Hulk, they needed Daryl Williams Jr. I couldn't take what worked in someone else's classroom and apply it directly to my students.

The same thing goes with these affirmations. Your students have very specific needs that may not be the same needs as others even within the same building. For that reason, here is a framework to create positive affirmations for the students in your class. Teaching your students to recite a daily affirmation will build that confidence they need to be capable of achieving the milestones you set before them.

Step 1: Address the Needs

First, ask yourself the question, **"What three things are holding my students back from achieving their full potential?"** Identify and attack the three key characteristics that might hinder your students' potential. Let's imagine that your students are constantly late to class, focus on the things that don't matter, and are easily distracted. Address these attributes in the first person, as if they're already achieved. In this example, you may create an affirmation similar to this:

"I am always on time to class, and when I get there, I can focus on

*the things that really matter, and
when distractions try to take my
attention, I don't lose focus."*

Step 2: Keep it Brief

While conveying the necessary information, strive for brevity. Deliver the message efficiently, ensuring it's both informative and engaging. Avoid overloading them with lengthy affirmations that may deter memorization. You may modify the affirmation to be something like this:

*"I am punctual, focusing on priorities, and
disregarding distractions."*

Step 3: Make it Catchy

Employ words that captivate and resonate. Utilize catchy phrases, rhymes, alliteration, or a rhythmic cadence. Crafting memorable affirmations encourages students to repeat and embrace them, fostering a positive attitude. You may settle on an affirmation like this:

*"I am punctual.
I prioritize tasks to be productive in class.
I keep the main thing the main thing, and
distractions don't phase me."*

Bonus: Be Consistent

Consistency is key. Incorporate the affirmation ritual into daily class routines. Starting each day with these affirmations reinforces their positive impact and creates a lasting habit.

As educators, we hold the power to rewrite the narratives our students internalize. Overcoming years of self-doubt and negative influences, we aim to cultivate an environment where self-affirmation and belief are fundamental.

Below are some affirmations to help you get started. Use these to spark your creativity process, but don't limit it to these. Allow your natural creativity to invent new affirmations that inspire them. The only rule for an affirmation is that it must be stated in the positive and must relate to the students individually rather than others. We cannot control the actions of others; we can only condition our own minds toward positivity:

I am capable of achieving great things.

I believe in my abilities to overcome challenges.

I am resilient and can learn from my mistakes.

I embrace new challenges as opportunities to grow.

I am in control of my own learning journey.

I am confident in my unique strengths and talents.

I am a problem solver and can find solutions to any challenge.

I am open to learning from others and expanding my knowledge.

I am determined and won't give up when faced with difficulties.

I am worthy of success and happiness.

I am constantly improving and progressing in my studies.

I am focused, motivated, and ready to tackle my goals.

I am not defined by my past; I am shaping my future.

I am responsible for my own success and actions.

I am adaptable and can thrive in any situation.

I am kind, capable, and full of potential.

I am confident in my abilities to learn and achieve.

I am a lifelong learner, always seeking to improve.

I am strong, and I can overcome any obstacle.

I am creating a better future for myself through hard work and dedication.

I am building skills now to create choices later.

I am living the life I choose, not the life I'm forced to settle for.

Using positive student affirmations is critical to making sure that students believe in themselves as much as you do. The side that we have yet to address in this impact triangle, is the parents. When students, teachers, and parents are all working together toward a common goal, the possibilities are endless. In the next chapter, we will learn how to communicate with parents effectively.

Chapter 19:
Communicate with
Parents Effectively

"If you just communicate, you
can get by. But if you
communicate skillfully, you can
work miracles."
– Jim Rohn

Communication is perhaps our greatest tool as teachers. To be honest, it is the same for all humans in all walks of life. Communication is what connects us. As teachers, we have to communicate with teachers, parents, coworkers, and superiors. The group that some teachers struggle with engaging effectively is parents.

Studies done by Waterford Upstart show that students who have teachers and parents that engage in one-to-one conversations are more likely to earn higher grades, participate in class, and feel positive about school. They are also less likely to need disciplinary consequences, fail classes, and to experience high stress levels means that students of parents and teachers that don't have that interaction are far more likely to do the exact opposite. So, they fail classes at a higher rate, misbehave more, and feel more stressed about school.

In previous chapters as we covered the art of creating visions, dreams, and goals, you probably discovered a multitude of aspirations for this school year. Realizing these ambitions requires a cohesive and collective effort, involving not only the teachers but also the students, families, and parents. It is essential for everyone to collaborate harmoniously, united by a shared objective, to make these dreams a reality. Working together, we can build a supportive and nurturing environment conducive to success.

I have organized my parent communication tips into three tiers for your convenience. First, I'll cover preventative measures. Next, I'll address conflict resolution. Finally, I'll tell you what to do when interactions verge on becoming dangerous. Additionally, I'll provide an overview of some general practices to consider.

Tier One: Preventative Measures

Sun Tzu, a renowned general, once wisely stated that the battle is won before it's even fought. This principle applies not only to warfare but also to communication. Effective communication begins with planning and preparation, much before any actual conversation takes place. If you invest time in planning and preparing before reaching out to parents, especially when addressing classroom issues or concerns, the communication process becomes significantly smoother.

In the context of the school system, let's borrow a concept from the business world: "People do business with people they **know, like,** and **trust**." Similarly, parents would prefer their children to be in classes with teachers they **know, like,** and **trust**. To foster effective communication throughout the academic year and minimize the need for challenging conversations, it's essential to build that connection with parents.

Begin by introducing yourself to get them to **know** you. This does not have to be anything elaborate, but it does have to be intentional. This can be as extravagant as hand delivering personalized gift baskets to each child's home (not recommended) or as simple as sending a newsletter with a brief bio. The main principle here is that you begin to build a positive relationship by allowing parents to get to know you.

Then, two great ways to get them to **like** you, are to give genuine compliments, and connect with them on shared interests or experiences. Be sure to give safe and appropriate compliments that won't land you in a Title IX investigation, but just make people feel special. You can say something like, "Joel is extremely well mannered. You're doing an amazing job at home." Compliments like this go a long way. Another way to get parents to like you is by connecting over shared interests. Find some things that you have in common and talk about them. I am an NFL fan, so whenever I see a parent with a Cowboys t-shirt, or a Dolphins license plate, I spark up a conversation. We talk about how the season is going, and since I am a Philadelphia Eagles fan, we talk about how my team is so much better than their team. They often admit to our superiority and I encourage them to keep their heads up. (Fly Eagles, Fly). Creating a positive and relatable relationship with parents will significantly enhance communication and cooperation, leading to a more supportive and successful learning environment.

Getting parents to **trust** you is the trickiest of the three. To get parents to trust you, you have to be able to prove that all of your decisions are with the best interest of their child in mind. Get them to trust you by sharing your vision. Remember, a vision is what you want to see happen for 100% of your students. When you communicate a vision that encompasses the success and well-being of all your students, parents will trust that their child is also a priority. Demonstrating that you have their best interests in mind fosters trust and confidence in your abilities to do what's best for each student.

Tier Two: Resolving Conflicts

Let's move on to Tier two, which focuses on resolving conflicts. To illustrate this, consider a scenario where a parent expresses concern that her son, Joel, comes home upset because he isn't chosen as the line leader every day. I know that I prefaced this section by saying that we would be dealing with Middle School students, and yes, I can confirm that this is a Middle School issue. It is real that a twelve-year-old can be upset about not being chosen to be the line leader, and then go home and complain about it to his *girlfriend* on face time all night. Welcome to Middle School.

When addressing such situations, the first step is to genuinely listen to the parent's main issue. Whether it's through phone calls, texts, or emails, it's vital to pay attention and grasp the core concern. In written communication, it's best to limit the back-and-forth to two or three exchanges and then consider picking up the phone to ensure clear understanding since tone can be hard to convey via text.

In this case, it's essential to recognize that the parent's true concern is not solely about Joel being the line leader every day. Instead, her primary worry is that he comes home upset due to this issue. In response, a suitable approach would be to acknowledge her concern and actively listen. You could say, "Okay, so what I'm hearing you say is that you don't want Joel to come home upset because he's not the line leader every single day." By paraphrasing her concern, you demonstrate empathy and validate her perspective, which lays the groundwork for constructive problem-solving and resolution.

The next step is to avoid shifting the blame. In situations where we feel attacked, it's essential to remember that parents are not attacking us personally;

they merely want what's best for their child. Even if it may seem like they are attacking us, reframing the perspective can be helpful. Instead of interpreting it as a personal attack, view it as their genuine concern for their child's well-being.

Avoid blaming the child for the situation, as this might seem evasive. Saying something like, "He needs to grow up" won't be effective in addressing the issue. Instead, respond empathetically by acknowledging their feelings. For instance, you can say, "Okay, I can understand how that makes you feel. I can see why you'd be upset that your child is coming home upset every day." By expressing understanding and validation, you show that you are open to their perspective without admitting wrongdoing. This approach can lead to more constructive and positive communication and ultimately facilitate conflict resolution.

As you transition into the next part and aim to become solution-oriented, it's essential to avoid using the word "but." Using "but: in transitions can inadvertently downplay the sincerity of your apology or empathy. Instead, consider incorporating a phrase like "I'd also like to add…" Here are two examples to illustrate the impact of using 'but':

> *Example with 'but'*: "I understand why that would upset you, for Joel to come home upset every day, but he was just a line leader yesterday. He needs to take turns.

Example without 'but': *"I understand why that would upset you, for Joel to come home upset every day. I would also like to add that a huge classroom core principle is that we provide opportunities for various students to take on different roles."*

By avoiding "but," you maintain the empathy expressed earlier while adding a rationale to support your approach towards a solution.

As you conclude the conversation, reinforce your genuine concern for the child's well-being. For instance, you might say, "While I would love for Joel to be the line leader every single day, my goal in class is to help students." This reminder underscores your commitment to the child's growth and future success, aligning with your vision for all students' development.

As you present a solution, it's crucial to maintain fairness and equity. Avoid singling out one child and granting them special treatment that you can't offer to everyone else. For instance, don't say, "Okay, I'll let him be the line leader every day," if it's not something you can do for all students. This approach may lead to gossip among students and parents, creating a perception of favoritism. To ensure fairness, ensure that the solution you provide is one that can be applied universally to any student in a similar situation. This way, you uphold a consistent and equitable learning environment for all.

Lastly, ensure that your solution directly addresses the main issue of the child being upset. Your proposed solutions should focus on alleviating their feelings of distress. For example, you might say, "I'll ensure that every time I select the line leader, I communicate how that person was chosen, and I'll make sure all students understand that they will have an opportunity at another time, so he's not so upset."

Tier Three: Exiting a Dangerous Situation

In most cases, the solutions we discussed earlier will suffice. However, we must acknowledge that conflicts can escalate, and there may be instances where potentially dangerous situations need to be addressed.

While I emphasize face-to-face or zoom conversations over phone calls and emails whenever possible, it's essential to ensure your safety during one-on-one interactions with parents. If you are in-person, always have a clear path to the exit. I don't want you to seem paranoid but prioritize your well-being. Position yourself in a way that allows easy access to the exit if needed.

If a conversation starts to escalate and feels potentially dangerous, it doesn't necessarily mean it will lead to physical altercations. It might simply mean that emotions are running high, and regrettable words could be exchanged. Before it reaches that point, a great strategy is to acknowledge that you don't have an immediate resolution, but you are willing to work on finding one. In such cases, suggest bringing in an administrator to mediate the discussion. You could say something like, "At this moment, I don't have a solution to the problem, but I believe it would be best to involve an administrator to help us work through this. Once they're available, we can reschedule a time to communicate and work together towards a resolution." This approach works both virtually, and in person, and shows that you prioritize finding a resolution and involving the appropriate support to ensure a productive and safe outcome.

Implementing this approach offers several advantages that can significantly improve the situation. First, it provides a much-needed break for all parties involved. When conflicts start to escalate, tensions can run high, and emotions may cloud rational thinking. Stepping away for a short recess, whether it's just five minutes while waiting for the administrator to arrive or rescheduling the meeting for a couple of days, allows everyone to cool off and gain perspective.

Secondly, involving an administrator introduces a fresh and impartial perspective into the conversation. Often, when disagreements arise, both parties can become entrenched in their positions, making it challenging to find common ground. By bringing in a neutral third party, such as an administrator, you introduce someone who can view the situation objectively and mediate the discussion more effectively. Their alternate perspective can shed new light on the matter, presenting ideas or solutions that the individuals involved may not have initially considered.

Furthermore, this approach shows a willingness to work towards a resolution and highlights the importance of seeking professional guidance when needed. It reflects a commitment to ensuring a fair and productive outcome for all parties involved.

Overall, taking this approach not only allows for a brief moment of reflection and regrouping but also brings in valuable external input to guide the conversation towards a more constructive and beneficial resolution. It emphasizes the significance of open communication, collaboration, and seeking additional perspectives to foster a supportive and harmonious learning environment for students and parents alike.

Now that you know how to communicate with parents effectively, you are in prime position to increase student achievement. The greatest way to see individual student growth is to differentiate the learning experience. The way we can do that is through small group instruction. In the next chapter, learn all about how to effectively implement small group instruction.

Chapter 20: Small Groups in Middle School

Far from being a detriment to student learning, differentiated instruction is the only way we can teach all students, not just the easy ones.

-Rick Wormeli

Small groups are so elementary, right? Not necessarily! Not only can small groups work in middle school and high school, but they should be used if you really want to accelerate student growth.

It's a well-known fact that students in any given classroom are not all at the same academic level, which shouldn't come as a surprise. However, the challenge lies in the traditional instructional approaches that often focus on catering to just one group of students. While this approach may benefit the targeted group, it inadvertently neglects other students who also deserve the opportunity to accelerate their academic growth.

In a diverse classroom, every student has unique learning needs, abilities, and potential for growth. By solely concentrating on one group, we unintentionally leave others behind, hindering their progress and limiting their chances of reaching their full potential. It's like feeding a few hungry students while neglecting others who also deserve nourishment to thrive academically.

This isn't groundbreaking information. It is common sense that different students have different needs. The reason why some teachers don't attempt small group instruction is not because they don't believe in its efficacy, but because of the pressure of proper preparation. Based on my research, there are three major roadblocks to small group instruction. I am first going to address these three roadblocks, then share the plan that I have found to be effective in helping maximize individual growth.

Three Major Roadblocks to Small Group Instruction

Classroom Management

A common concern I often hear from Middle School teachers regarding small group instruction is the management issue. They wonder how they can effectively manage a classroom with 30-plus hormone charged, emotionally distressed, adolescent students when simultaneously implementing small groups. The fear of dealing with multiple groups engaged in various activities - while potentially talking about inappropriate topics, leaving their seats, and licking things - can be overwhelming. It seems impractical to dedicate oneself to one group while chaos ensues in other areas. This seems like a good time to remind you that you've got to practice how you intend to perform. In order to perform small groups well, you've got to practice small groups well. Before delving into standards-based content while in small groups, I encourage teachers to take the time to practice and familiarize themselves with what small group instruction should look like in their classroom.

To begin the practice phase, divide your students into groups and provide them with independent tasks to work on. Depending on the time of the year, you can choose activities like "All About Me" at the beginning of the year or "Mindset Development" such as what can be found in the Choices Curriculum, later in the year. Another option is to have them share their dreams or visions for the class. Whatever activity you decide on, the key is to ensure these activities can be completed independently, allowing you to focus solely on classroom management.

As the students work in their groups, move around the classroom and address specific issues as needed. For instance, you might remind one group to lower their voices if the small group discussions get too loud. Let them engage in a few small group activities, spanning a couple of class periods or days. This process may take time to roll out effectively, but the main focus during this phase should be on managing the small groups efficiently. The goal here is not just to practice until they get it right, practice until they can't get it wrong.

After you get the management down, after you get to the point where you can put them in small groups and you could just sit down if you wanted to for 20, 30 minutes, and they would continue moving like a well-oiled machine, then you introduce the content into the small group activities.

Classroom Culture

Another concern in utilizing small group instruction is that it would highlight the deficiencies in some students. That can be the case if not implemented correctly. But as the leader of the classroom, it is your job to make sure that students don't see differences as deficiencies. It is your job to make sure that the classroom culture is one built on acceptance and support. It's crucial to understand that this approach is not about segregating students based on ability or creating divisions within the class. Instead, it's about providing targeted support and individualized instruction to meet the unique needs of each student. By addressing specific learning gaps and misconceptions, you are ensuring that every student has the opportunity to succeed at their own pace. Students must accept that we are all different, and have various needs, and be willing to support each other as we all work towards the common goal.

You do this by being transparent about the fact that we all have different needs, and that you care about them way too much to ignore their needs. Let them know that if you didn't care, you would ignore their needs and just have a universal approach to learning. You would just throw information out there and whoever caught it, caught it. But you care way too much about them and their individual growth to do that. You care way too much to just send them on to the next grade without fully maximizing their potential in this one. And because you care that much, you are making it your mission to individualize the learning experience. Let them know that in order to do it effectively you need their help. You need them to recognize that other students will be working on different activities from time to time, and that is because what they are doing is exactly what they need to grow. Let them know that their roles as students is not to compare themselves to anyone else, but to focus on being the best version of themselves. The only way we all win is if we each win. So, let's allow each other to win.

One strategy to help protect some of the judgmental comparisons is to name the groups something other than "High" "Medium" and "Low." Try naming them something that goes along with your theme that we created in Chapter 8. Early in my career I had a "Zero Gravity" theme (because although sometimes we get knocked down, we refused to stay down). I decorated the room like outer space, with stars and other intergalactic graphics around the room. My groups could then be planet names, or solar systems, or rocket ships. So instead of saying, "the high group is working on Blooket and the low group is working on this fact fluency worksheet," you can say, "Venus is working on Blooket, and Mars is working on the worksheet on the back table." This type of nomenclature protects the achievement levels of the individuals in each group.

Once groups are in full effect, then be very vigilant for those that try to compare themselves to others. Whether they are laughing at students working on "easier" tasks, or discouraged because they see others working on more rigorous tasks, address the situation as soon as it arises. Don't take this lightly, because if it goes ignored, it will create a toxic culture. In the next chapter we will go in depth about how to deal with students falling short of behavioral expectations.

Difficulty of Planning

Another reason why teachers avoid utilizing small group instruction is because of the amount of work it takes to plan. Here is how you keep that from being a burden. Leverage the resources that you already have and predetermine what each group will work on. You don't need to create everything from scratch or buy it from Teachers Pay Teachers. You may already have access to workbooks, laptops, tablets, leftover curriculum, and assignments from other teacher in the building. Utilize those resources to help support your instruction. Perhaps one group is on laptops, while another is working in the workbook, and the final group is doing an activity you copied out of the leftover summer school curriculum books. There are many possibilities.

When you decide on the activities, include the directions for each group in the presentation for the day. That way, when it is time for small group work, you can just point to the board/screen and students can follow the directions pertaining to their group. This is a game changer because in the moment, you aren't scrambling, trying to explain what to do. Rather, you are just making sure each student knows what group they are in, and they can take it from there. It makes the transition smoother.

Small Group Implementation

Now that we have gotten rid of the roadblocks that were in our way, now we can dive into to structure of effective small groups in Middle School classrooms. This is the way I have seen be successful.

On small group instruction days in a 45- to 70-minute block, your lesson should not exceed 15 minutes. Once you deliver your concise lesson, it's time for a lesson check. This step is not the exit ticket; instead, it helps you assess whether the students grasped the concepts you just taught. Some students may immediately understand and can proceed to practice and develop their skills independently. Others might have grasped most of the content but still need further clarification on certain points before feeling confident to move forward. And, of course, there will be some students who are completely lost; this is a normal occurrence.

The key is to perform the lesson check at this stage to determine which students are ready to progress, who needs some clarification, and who requires more support. This assessment will help you categorize students into different groups based on their understanding.

For those students who have mastered the material, they can move on to work independently or collaboratively, depending on your preference. They are prepared to tackle new challenges confidently.

Students who need further clarification on specific concepts can work together in a group. Provide them with additional practice problems similar to the ones you just covered. You might have them review their notes or revisit the lesson slides to address any misconceptions or gaps in their understanding. Focusing on these particular points will ensure they are fully prepared before moving forward.

For the third group of students, who are significantly struggling, the approach is different. Dedicate your time to working closely with them, helping them trace back to where the confusion began. I like to call it the "jump-off" point. This "jump-off point" is the point at which they started to lose their grasp on the material. Think about it like a plane that is going down, and the student has a parachute. Even with a parachute, it's pretty scary to jump out of a plane. But at some point, it makes more sense to jump-off with a parachute, than it does to go down with the plane. At what point did the student "jump-off" of your lesson? It could even be a concept from a previous grade level, and that's perfectly fine. Spend time with this group, pinpointing the source of their confusion, and address it directly during the small group session.

It is essential to float around the classroom and not solely focus on one group. While providing support to students who need it is crucial, you should also check in with higher-achieving students, address their questions, and continue to challenge them. Ensuring that all students are on track, even when working independently, is equally important. High achievers may also benefit from occasional guidance and encouragement to stay focused and avoid distractions.

By customizing your approach and providing targeted support to each group, you create a dynamic learning environment that caters to individual needs. This tailored instruction ensures that all students receive the appropriate guidance, allowing them to progress effectively in their learning journey.

Towards the end of the class, after the small group sessions, it's essential to conduct an actual exit ticket that aligns with the standards you covered, much like the lesson check earlier. This exit ticket serves as a follow-up assessment, aimed at identifying which students have grasped the concepts, who still needs some clarification, and who may still be struggling.

By conducting this exit ticket, you gain valuable insights into the students' progress and understanding. You can determine which students have confidently grasped the material, who may need some additional support or clarification, and who might still be facing challenges. This information becomes instrumental in planning for the next day's lesson.

Based on the exit ticket results, you can make informed decisions about the content and pacing for the following day's instruction. For example, students who have demonstrated a strong understanding of protons may be ready to move on to electrons. For those who need further clarification, you can modify your approach to ensure they have a solid foundation before progressing. And for students who are still struggling, you can plan targeted interventions to address their specific needs.

Incorporating the exit ticket as part of your instructional practice allows you to continually monitor student progress and adjust your teaching accordingly. This individualized approach ensures that all students receive the support they require to reach their learning goals effectively. It fosters a dynamic and responsive learning environment, empowering each student to build a strong foundation of knowledge and confidently progress through the curriculum.

Once you have administered the exit ticket, you might wonder how to determine the right time to move on to the next topic. The following is the rubric that I adhere to. Read closely to understand the rationale behind the breakdown, and feel free to adjust the percentages to be applicable to your school community.

To move on to the next topic, look for a sign that approximately 70% of your students have demonstrated mastery over the content taught in today's lesson. This 70% threshold is meaningful because it allows for a continuous cycle of reinforcement and revisiting concepts. You'll have ample opportunities to reinforce the material through warm-ups, launch activities, homework, and practice exercises.

The reason you don't need 100% mastery at this point is that ongoing practice and reiteration will help solidify the understanding for all students, including the remaining 30% who might not have achieved mastery yet. The focus is on ensuring that the majority of the class is proficient, and you can then dedicate your attention to supporting those who need additional assistance.

By using this 70% benchmark, you strike a balance between moving forward in the curriculum and ensuring comprehensive learning for your entire class. As you progress, you'll remain mindful of the 30% who may still need support, providing targeted help and interventions to help them catch up.

If 50% to 60% of your students show mastery on the exit ticket, it's time to pause and exercise caution. This percentage indicates that a significant portion of your class still holds misconceptions about the material covered in today's lesson. In this situation, it's advisable not to proceed full steam ahead. Instead, consider dedicating some time during the next lesson to address these common misconceptions promptly.

Take the opportunity to clarify the misunderstandings and conduct another assessment to gauge if the students are now ready to move forward. It's crucial not to rush ahead with only half of the class fully understanding the content. Ensuring that a majority of students have a strong grasp of the material is essential for effective learning.

If less than 50% of your students demonstrate mastery on the exit ticket, it's essential to stop and reassess the situation. This scenario indicates that more than half of your class is still confused, and proceeding with the next lesson would not be responsible teaching practice. Instead, acknowledge that the lesson may not have been as successful as intended, and that's alright.

As a conscientious educator, you should own the situation and make adjustments accordingly. Take the necessary time to address the areas of confusion, revisit the material, and provide additional support as needed. By doing so, you create a supportive and nurturing learning environment, allowing every student to progress at their own pace and achieve the desired level of understanding.

When you encounter students who are still struggling with a particular concept, it's essential to address the issue in the next session. At this point, take a decisive pause, revisit the standard you covered, and consider breaking it down into smaller chunks. For instance, if you were teaching adding and subtracting with scientific notation, focus solely on adding first, and then tackle subtraction separately at a later time. This approach ensures that you don't proceed to more advanced topics like multiplying and dividing with scientific notation until the students have grasped the fundamentals.

If you're skeptical about whether this approach will work with your students, I strongly encourage you to give it a try. There's no harm in attempting something new. "Oh wells" are far better than "what ifs." If you never put it into practice, you'll never find out. Taking action and trying out this strategy is the key to discovering its potential.

Of course, there's a chance it might not yield the desired results, and that's okay. If it doesn't work, you can simply move on to explore other strategies. The important thing is to take the leap and try. Embrace the possibility of failure, as it paves the way for growth and learning.

However, what if you do try it and it turns out to be successful? That's an incredible achievement! Taking risks and trying new methods can lead to amazing outcomes, and that's why I encourage you to go for it wholeheartedly.

In the end, it's about being proactive and open to exploring new approaches in your teaching. Don't let doubts hold you back; instead, embrace the 'Oh Wells' and seize the opportunity to make a positive impact on your students' learning journey. Be bold, be innovative, and let curiosity guide you. You never know what great things may come from taking that leap of faith.

Chapter 21: Classroom Management Systems

The key to classroom behavior management is to have a structured system in place whereby good behaviors are actively and abundantly rewarded, and bad behaviors are promptly and efficiently punished. Rewards should be like the air, ever present and always lingering. Punishment should be like a thunderstorm that is obvious and inconvenient yet quick, temporary and not abusive.

-Hendrith Vanlon Smith Jr

Dealing with a constantly noisy class can be frustrating and detrimental to effective teaching. With the challenges students face in education globally, it's crucial not to let them fall behind. The noise in the classroom can be embarrassing and disheartening, as it disrupts the learning environment. As a former terrible teacher, I can relate to being in that situation, where neighboring teachers had to intervene to quiet down my students so their classes could focus. The teacher from next door would come over and say, "You all are entirely too loud!" And I would just stand there like a puppy getting scolded and say, "I tried to tell them." I understand how uncomfortable and undesirable that can be.

To help you avoid such situations, I'd like to share some valuable tips for regaining control and quieting your noisy class. By implementing these strategies, you can create a conducive learning environment and ensure that your students receive the education they deserve without constant distractions. Let's work together to create a positive and productive classroom experience for both you and your students.

1. Clear Expectations. Consistent Consequences.

To effectively address behavioral issues in your classroom, the first step is to establish clear expectations and maintain consistent consequences. A pivotal moment in my teaching journey was when I decided to display a sign on the back wall of my class that read, "Clear Expectations, Consistent Consequences." This visual reminder helped me stay focused on the key elements that would elevate my classroom management. During my initial struggles as a teacher, I realized that I was sometimes responding to misbehavior based on my emotions rather than the students' actions.

To overcome this, I set explicit expectations for behaviors. Expectations work better than rules, because rules are negatively framed, and can never address every behavior. For example, a classroom rule might be, "Don't get out of your seat without permission" A few weeks into the school year, a student might slide in their chair across the floor to other side of the classroom where their friend is, look at you with a smile and say, "I didn't get out of my seat!" We know these students. A better approach would be to have an expectation like, "Be Productive." Now, I don't care if you walk, slide, glide, or fly across the classroom, you are falling short of the expectation and will receive a consequence. My four expectations are always:

1. Be Prompt
2. Be Productive
3. Be Professional
4. Be Positive

I know that my class will run smoothly if all students adhere to all four expectations. I'll show you how it works. Students are considered to be misbehaving when they are doing something that doesn't meet an expectation. Since we have an expectation to Be Professional, we respect other's learning opportunities by maintaining a voice level of zero for complete silence during instruction. By doing so, any deviation from this expectation, whether it was a whisper or shouting, was recognized as falling short. Early in my career, I made the mistake of only giving consequences when students were shouting, while ignoring minor infractions like whispers. This inconsistency created a perception of unfairness among my students. To rectify this, I learned to apply consistent consequences for any deviation from the established expectations.

It all starts with clearly defining the expectations. For instance, when we are at voice level zero, it means complete silence like a pin-drop across the class. At voice level one, students know they can communicate with a whisper to their neighbor but cannot shout across the room. Communicate these expectations clearly to your students as you transition into different parts of the day and ensure that every student who doesn't adhere to these expectations receives the same consequences. This consistency fosters a fair and respectful learning environment where all students understand the rules and expectations and can focus on their education without disruptions.

The Five-Tiered System

My preferred consequence system incorporates a five-tiered approach to address misbehavior effectively. It begins with a warning, followed by a loss of teacher-controlled privilege, a seat change, parent contact, and ultimately, taking a break in another classroom with another teacher.

Warning

The warning should be stated clearly and directly align to the expectation that is not being met. It does not need to be a big deal, or a power struggle. Notice the behavior, state the student's name, remind of the expectation, assign the warning, and move on.

Loss of Teacher-Controlled Privilege

The emphasis here is the "teacher-controlled" portion. It is always best practice to administer consequences that you can control. Things like, afterschool detention, running laps, and even silent lunch are not my preferred consequences because one, some of those methods are illegal, and two, they all require students to comply. You can't control whether a student can stay for afterschool detention, or if they choose to not talk during silent lunch. For this reason, I suggest things like taking away a point, access to a reward, money earned in the class economy system, etc. Something that you as the teacher can control, and the student has no say in the matter. Take away the privilege and move on.

Seat Change

If the student is still misbehaving, a shift in environment may be helpful. A great idea here is to have a predetermined "isolation station" or "reflection section" where students go when they receive this consequence. You may notice that this is not teacher controlled, as the student may refuse to move. That's fine, you are prepared for this. In these instances, my go to is to move the audience from around that student.

But Mr. Williams, they didn't do anything wrong. They don't deserve to move.

I know, and you're right! I always say something like this:

"Megan, the expectation right now is a voice level zero, but you are singing. Go ahead and take a seat in the reflection section."

Megan rolls her eyes and ignores me.

"Ok. Nyelle, can you do me a favor and move over to the seat next to Joel? You aren't in trouble. I just care way too much about you and your learning to have you forced to be seated at a table where you are constantly distracted. Thank you."

And move on.

Parent Contact + Student Conference

If the student continues, then the next step in the tiered system is to contact the parent. Perhaps it's a phone call, but it can also be an email, a Parentsquare message, a carrier pigeon, however you want to contact them. The student conference can be a quick kneel down next to the desk, or a conversation in the hallway, but the phrase I always use during the conference is this:

"Megan, you haven't been making the best decisions so far today. At this point, I am definitely going to contact your grownups after class, but you get to decide what I say. Either I will say, Megan had a rough day today, or I can say, 'Megan started off a little rocky, but we had a conversation and she turned it around.' The choice is yours."

Offer her a two-minute water break to refocus herself, welcome her back into the classroom community, and move on.

Take a Break in Another Classroom

The final step in this system before involving administration, is to send the student to another classroom. For this to work, you first need to coordinate with a buddy teacher to make sure that they are willing to take a student of yours. Once that is squared away, make sure that the student is sent with work to complete, and for a predetermined amount of time. My go to is fifteen minutes. Let the buddy teacher know that their role is not to have to manage the student, just monitor. That being said, if the student is causing disruptions in the buddy class, that would be a good time to involve administration because the behaviors have transcended just your classroom. If they last all fifteen minutes in the buddy classroom, welcome them back into the classroom, and move on.

If they are still falling short of the expectations, then involve administration. At this point, you have done your due diligence, and the student has become a detriment to all others in the classroom, and that is not fair.

The goal of the consequence system is not to punish but to teach. It's not about finding harsh or outlandish punishments; rather, it aims to guide students in understanding and adhering to appropriate behavior. We don't seek to harm or hurt the students but to offer them opportunities for growth and learning.

This tiered system provides multiple chances for students to recognize and rectify their missteps, reminding them at each phase that their behavior is unacceptable.

2. Handle Issues on Your Own

Another essential tip is to handle classroom issues yourself instead of constantly involving administrators. Here is the best way I know how to put it. I am the eldest of four children. My brother Dante is six years younger than me; my sister Dayani is eight years younger than me; and my brother Davier is twelve years younger than me. So, growing up, I was always given the responsibility of being in charge when my parents weren't around. For the most part, they were easy to manage, but every now and then I would give them a directive and they would remind me that I was not their parent. They would say things like, "I don't have to listen to you" or "you're not my Dad!" In those moments I would call one of my parents to tell on my siblings. In that moment, it got my sibling to do what they were supposed to do, but I learned that tattling on my younger siblings to our parents didn't foster a stronger bond between us; instead, it reinforced the authority our parents had in the situation. Similarly, in the classroom, if we consistently call on administrators to address issues, we inadvertently diminish our own authority and strengthen the perception that administrators have more control over the students.

This approach can lead to a disconnect between teachers and students.

Taking charge of the issues on your own helps maintain your authority as a teacher and builds a positive relationship with the students. It communicates to them that you are capable of handling challenges within the classroom and that you support their growth and learning. Escalate to administration only if necessary, after going through the five-tier system mentioned earlier. This system allows you to address behavioral concerns step by step, giving students opportunities to learn and rectify their actions before involving administrators.

In cases where a student has reached the end of the five tiers and still exhibits disruptive behavior, administration may need to intervene. However, after the issue is resolved, it's crucial to maintain a strong relationship with the student. Have relationship-building conversations with them and clarify that the goal is not to exclude them but to create a conducive learning environment for everyone in the class.

*It's important to note that the five-tier system is designed for behaviors that do not pose immediate risk or danger. For fights or other dangerous situations, it's necessary to involve administration without hesitation.

3. Attention Grabbing Signals

When attempting to quiet the class quickly, the goal is to capture your class's attention without having to raise your voice over the chatter. Instead of struggling to quiet down the room, you can implement a simple procedure to engage your students immediately. Something like a call-and-response, hand signal, Bluetooth doorbell chime, gong, etc., is critical for grabbing student's attention. My personal go-to is call-and-response.

You can make it fun and engaging by using phrases like "When I say dream, you say big! Dream! Big! Dream! Big!" or "Let there be peace," to which students respond "Let it begin with me." There are endless possibilities. You can even get creative with popular jingles like "Bada-ba-ba-ba," to which the class responds with "I'm lovin' it!" Or you can go the trendy route and say something like, "Look around, everybody on mute…" Sprinkle these call and response moments throughout the day to keep the atmosphere lively, and student attention focused.

The key is to practice it with your students so that they know when you use a specific phrase, they should respond immediately and then focus on you. The goal is to have 100% engagement after the attention getting signal. Similar to practicing the small group management, spend a considerable amount of time practicing how students should respond to the signal. You don't just want to practice until they get it right, practice until they can't get it wrong. This way, they understand that what follows is important, and they need to pay attention.

By incorporating attention-grabbing signals into your classroom routine, you create a dynamic and responsive learning environment where students are attentive and eager to participate in the lessons.

4. Positive Narration

Positive narration is an incredibly powerful tool that can transform your classroom dynamics. When we hear the term "positive narration," we might picture a kindergarten teacher using a cute voice to praise Joel for sitting crisscross-applesauce on the carpet. However, it doesn't have to be that way.

Positive narration simply involves naming the behavior you want to see and recognizing students who demonstrate it. It's about making the expectation clear and celebrating those who meet it. You don't have to resort to baby talk or over-the-top expressions. Instead, let your students know that you're observant and you notice when they follow the classroom expectations.

Positive narration can come into play with the attention-grabbing signal as well. After using a call and response, acknowledge and praise the students who responded well, saying something like, "This is awesome! Look at this table sitting silently and paying attention. I see you, Nyelle, being focused and locked in!"

By publicly acknowledging students who behave according to the expectations, you create a positive atmosphere that encourages others to follow suit. It becomes a popular choice to align with the desired behavior because students appreciate the recognition and approval from their teacher. Positive narration reinforces the idea that meeting expectations is admirable and fosters a sense of pride and accomplishment among the students.

So, as you practice positive narration in your classroom, remember to keep it genuine and age-appropriate. Praise the positive behaviors you want to see more of and watch as the desired behavior becomes the norm in your classroom.

5. Short and Engaging Lesson

This tip focuses on keeping your lessons brief, engaging, and within the attention span of your students, which is typically no more than 15 minutes. To achieve this, remember the phrase "be brief, be bright, be fun, be done." Avoid extending direct-instruction lessons beyond 15 minutes at one time, as students' attention wanes, and they may start talking or becoming restless. If a lesson requires more time, consider breaking it into shorter segments and teaching those parts separately at different times. To stick with the example from Chapter 20, let's say you plan to teach Adding and Subtracting with Scientific Notation and you anticipate it taking 25 minutes. Instead of one 25-minute lesson, try a 12-minute lesson on Adding with Scientific Notation, practice, and then a 12-minute lesson on Subtracting with Scientific Notation, followed by practice. This helps students remain engaged, and also helps retain information.

To further increase retention and engagement within the lesson, even the 15-minute lesson can be segmented into chunks.

During these segments, alternate between teacher-led instruction and student interaction. For example, in a 5-minute block, you would spend around 4 minutes delivering the content, followed by a period of time, up to 1 minute for students to reflect and respond to questions. Some of my favorite quick reflection phrases are as follows:

- Turn to your partner and summarize what we have learned so far.
- What is a question that you have, or that someone else in the class might have?
- Tell the class what I just said, but in your own words.
- What would happen if we _____ instead of _____ when working on problems like this?
- In exactly six words, summarize the key point of the lesson so far.
- What is something we are doing well as a class so far today?

This four-to-one teacher talk to student talk ratio encourages students to actively participate in the learning process. Providing these reflection breaks allows students to process the information, retain key concepts, and solidify their understanding of the material. Be diligent about adhering to the 4-minute teaching intervals and allow students ample time to share their thoughts, ask questions, and engage in discussions.

But Mr. Williams, that's unrealistic to stop exactly every four minutes while I'm delivering my lesson.

For some it is, for some it's not. I like to say the 4:1 ratio is not an exact science, but a general rule of thumb. To simply put it, there should be three opportunities within the 15-minute lesson where you stop and encourage students to reflect. Make it clear, keep it brief, and get back into the lesson. This approach not only keeps students focused and attentive but also empowers them to take an active role in their learning journey. By incorporating these reflective moments, you create a dynamic and interactive learning environment that fosters deeper comprehension and meaningful connections with the subject matter.

By respecting your students' attention spans and providing opportunities for reflection and engagement, you'll foster a more attentive and participative class, leading to fewer disruptions and a more productive learning experience.

6. Keep them Engaged

Ensure that students always have engaging tasks to keep them on track throughout the class. When students have idle time, they may become disinterested, and student disinterest leads to student disruption. To avoid this, plan ahead and have additional activities or assignments ready for those who finish early. I actually got this idea from one of my High School teachers. I remember being in class and whenever someone said, "I'm Done!" she would respond with, "A steak can be done, you cannot. Go on to the next thing." I adopted this approach in my classes as well, making sure that there was always something for them to do next. Whether it was an acceleration activity, or a review activity, students knew once they finished one task where to go to find the next one. It did not involve me having to scramble in the moment to find something for them to do, and it definitely did not involve any type of "Free Time." Students would simply go into their binders or onto Google Classroom and continue on to the next assignment.

By proactively providing meaningful tasks for every student, you keep them focused and motivated throughout the class period. This approach not only prevents disruptions but also maximizes their learning opportunities. Whether it's extension activities, creative exercises, or review tasks, having something purposeful for each student to work on ensures that they stay productive and on-task for the entire duration of the class. Remember, an occupied mind is less likely to wander, so always be prepared to keep their minds engaged!

7. Communicate with Parents Effectively

Lastly, maintain constant communication with parents to keep them informed about their child's progress and any behavioral issues. Reflect on Chapter 19 to assist with this. Parents deserve to know if their child's behavior is impeding their learning, or if they are a model student. This information is very helpful for families. Also, as I mentioned in Chapter 19, students in classes where the teacher is in constant communication with their parents perform better academically. Keep that in mind as you seek to improve your classroom management systems.

Chapter 22: When Nothing Else Seem to Work... Try this

"Good classroom management is the art of dealing with problems positively and looking for solutions together so that everyone is involved and willing to find a remedy."

-Kavita Bhupta Ghosh

For the majority of your students (around 80% to 90%), setting clear expectations and applying consistent consequences, as mentioned in Chapter 21, will work to effectively manage the classroom. However, it's essential to acknowledge that there might be some students who prove to be exceptionally challenging and defiant, and the standard approach may not work for them. In this chapter, we will explore strategies to address and handle such situations with these students.

1. Clear Expectations. Consistent Consequences.

Keep the expectations consistent but be flexible on the activities. It is essential to ensure that the expectations for the entire class remain the same. If you start allowing students to get away with things, people will start to say that your system is flawed. The students won't fall in line because they'll wonder, "If other kids can get away with things, why can't I?"

Let's consider an example where you have an expectation that students should be productive in class. One day, a student named Marley falls asleep during the lesson, which is not productive and falls short of the expectation. When you address this, she responds positively to a warning and gets back on track.

Now, in the same class, there may be an extremely defiant student, Megan. Megan consistently refuses to do her work, ignores instructions, and typical consequences don't seem to have an impact on her behavior. She is also sleeping in class today. Dealing with Megan requires a different approach. Despite the different responses from Megan, you must still clearly state that the expectation is the same for all students. The rest of the class needs to be aware of this and believe that they will receive fair treatment.

You can address the class and say, "It seems like Megan has made her decision. She knows that sleeping in class is not acceptable. Megan, we'll meet during lunch or after school to ensure you get the notes you missed." Even if you need to apply different consequences for different students, it's crucial for the class to understand that consequences will be given when someone falls short of expectations. They need to know that Megan's behavior was addressed, even if the consequences were different for her. This approach maintains fairness and accountability in the classroom.

As the teacher, it can be frustrating to see Megan sleeping in class and being defiant about instructions. It might be tempting to get angry or upset, especially when she avoids eye contact and doesn't engage. However, you must remind yourself that Megan may be dealing with some difficult and traumatic experiences in her life, which could be influencing her behavior.

Instead of getting angry, choose to approach the situation with understanding and empathy. She may be going through a tough time, and you need to find a way to break through and connect with her. It's essential to be patient, compassionate, and open-minded as you work to understand her perspective and provide the support she needs to overcome any challenges she may be facing. By creating a supportive and caring environment, you can help Megan feel comfortable enough to open up and engage positively in the classroom.

2. Connect with Parents/Guardians

Establish connections with their guardians. When dealing with challenging students, it's crucial to reach out and connect with their grown-ups, whoever they may be. Even if you anticipate that some parents might be unresponsive or disengaged, communication with them remains essential. Keeping the grown-ups informed about the situation and your efforts to support their child is crucial.

Sometimes, it may seem daunting to talk to certain parents who appear difficult to communicate with, but it's still essential to engage with them. Ensure you maintain open lines of communication and let them know what is happening in the classroom and how you plan to assist their child. Building a partnership with the student's guardians can lead to a more holistic approach to helping the student succeed both academically and personally.

3. Communicate Your Vision

Communicate your vision to both the student and their guardians. Your vision represents what you want to see for all your students. Let them know that your ultimate goal is to help each student become the best version of themselves, even if the approach may differ for each individual. It's crucial that they understand that you are on their side, and are genuinely committed to their success.

A single speech may not be enough to completely turn things around, especially if they have been exposed to negative feedback for years. However, consistently conveying that you care, believe in their potential, and are willing to use a collaborative approach, can make a significant difference. Reassure them that they are full of potential and that you are determined to support them in getting back on track. When they truly feel your dedication to their growth, they will be more motivated to strive for improvement and become the best version of themselves.

4. Focus on the Positives

Focus on affirming their positive qualities. Avoid telling them what they are not, like saying they are "not bad" or "not dumb." Instead, emphasize the things that they truly are. Imagine if someone you were in a relationship with tried to connect with you by saying, "Out of everyone I've been with, you are not the ugliest." It wouldn't be very appealing. But when they say, "You are the most beautiful person I ever laid my eyes on," it makes all the difference. Similarly, when speaking to students, don't just say, "You're not a bad kid; you made a bad decision." Rather, emphasize, "You made a mistake, and that's okay. We all make mistakes. But truly exceptional people learn from them and move forward. I know you have the potential for greatness."

By shifting the focus to their strengths and positive attributes and encouraging them to learn from their mistakes and grow, you empower them to develop their potential and become better versions of themselves. Affirmations and positive reinforcement can go a long way in building their confidence and fostering a growth mindset. Revisit Chapter 18 for more about Positive Student Affirmations.

5. Find their Trusted Adult in the Building

Support them finding their trusted person, even if it's not you. It's essential to acknowledge that not every student will connect with you, and that's perfectly fine.

As a teacher, you might not be everyone's cup of tea. Some students may find someone else in the school whom they trust and can turn to for support, and that's a positive thing.

When I became a teacher, it was because I felt like I never had "my person" throughout school. Many teachers are inspired by educators they had in the past, but for me, I never had that special person. I love the quote by Tinku Razoria that says, "Everybody should have someone to whom they can tell the truth when asked, 'How are you?'" But I've come to understand that I might not be that person for everyone.

In those moments when a student like Megan is feeling anxious or defiant, and you can't figure out why you've got to learn to be okay with the fact that you might not be the one to solve that problem. You'll still have to teach her for the rest of the year, but if she finds someone else in the building, like Mrs. Pierce, whom she can trust and seek help from, that's a valuable resource. Allowing them to find that support system can make a significant difference in their lives and provide the help they need. It's about understanding that what matters most is supporting their well-being and academic growth, even if it means connecting with someone other than you.

6. Help Them to See Success

Foster their sense of success. This tip is one of my favorites. Many defiant students struggle academically or emotionally. They might feel discouraged by their grades or bored with the material. It's crucial to help them experience success in small ways, as it can boost their confidence and motivation to improve. Often, these students have been repeatedly told that they are bad or dumb, and they internalize a sense of failure. By showing them moments of success, we can create a desire for them to remain engaged in our class and continue to grow.

I recall a significant moment during my second Teacher of the Year observation when I had a challenging student. Let's continue to use the name Megan. She was known for her defiance and academic struggles. While being observed leading a lesson on The Pythagorean Theorem, my randomizer landed on Megan to answer a question. Recognizing whose name was highlighted, the class and observers held their collective breaths. Instead of avoiding the situation like most teachers might, I called on her and asked, "For what shape does the Pythagorean Theorem work?" The class sat silently in anticipation. Megan looked at me, looked at the cameras recording, looked at the shapes on the board, then looked back at me and responded, "A triangle?"

The class erupted in clapping and cheering.

I then went to another student and asked, "What type of triangle?" He replied, "Right triangle." And we continued with the lesson. It was a small win, but a meaningful one. By allowing Megan to experience success, I helped her feel smart and capable. It remains one of my proudest moments as a teacher.

In those moments, we must find opportunities for students to succeed, even in simple ways. Celebrating their accomplishments and showing them that they can do well in certain areas can make a significant difference in how they view themselves and their ability to learn. Encouraging a sense of success is what teaching is all about.

7. Build Strong Relationships

Lastly and probably most importantly, prioritize building relationships with your students. Take the time to get to know them, discover their interests, and try to connect with them over shared hobbies or passions. For example, if Megan enjoys cooking, you could challenge her to a friendly French toast cook-off. Even if you can't cook nearly quite as well as she can, the goal is to have fun and strengthen your relationship. Finding common ground and engaging in activities you both enjoy is incredibly valuable. Positive relationships can have a significant impact on their behavior and overall engagement in the classroom.

By implementing these tips, you can make considerable progress with even the most challenging students and help them become more involved and successful in their learning journey.

We explored earlier how students can sometimes be bonded to the trauma they have experienced in school. They may have been wounded in their past classroom situations by teachers who didn't use their powers for good. The system may have failed them. They may have had situations that cause them to lose their fire.

As a result, when you swoop in, full of energy, promising to save the day, those broken students don't always respond. Worse, many of them act out and disrupt your class.

The phrase "people don't care how much you know until they know how much you care" sums up a profound truth about human relationships, especially in the context of teaching and leadership. It emphasizes the importance of building genuine connections and fostering a sense of trust and empathy before attempting to impart knowledge or influence others and certainly before attempting to apply any kind of discipline.

In the realm of education, this concept underscores the significance of the teacher-student **relationship**. Yes, it's all about relationship. Students are more receptive to learning and are likely to be more engaged when they feel that their teacher truly cares about their well-being, growth, and success. When students sense that their teacher has their best interests at heart, they become more open to the learning process and are willing to take risks, ask questions, and embrace challenges.

Caring goes beyond simply expressing concern or offering support during difficult times. It involves demonstrating a sincere interest in each student as an individual, understanding their unique strengths, challenges, and aspirations. It means actively listening to their thoughts and feelings, showing empathy, and celebrating their successes, no matter how big or small.

When students feel cared for, they are more likely to be motivated to excel academically and behave positively in the classroom. They develop a sense of belonging and trust in their teacher's guidance, making it easier for the teacher to guide and challenge them in their learning journey.

This is true for all human beings, so why would it be any different in a classroom? People are more likely to follow and respect leaders who genuinely care about their well-being and success. Leaders who prioritize the welfare of their team members — students, in your case — build a sense of loyalty and commitment. This kind of caring leadership fosters a positive and supportive environment.

Be aware that this process won't occur overnight; it requires time and patience. Even though you have a well-structured curriculum and lesson plan, you might need to temporarily set it aside to address the formidable barrier that a student has built. This barrier is not intended to keep you out; it exists because the student didn't feel safe enough to let others in.

Before implementing disciplinary measures, take the time to understand the underlying factors that might be contributing to the student's behavior. Academic struggles, personal issues, or past trauma can significantly impact a student's attitude towards school and authority. Build a relationship with the student to gain insight into their perspective and experiences. I know they look like a smart aleck intent on defying everything you say. In reality, they are wounded and afraid. Everything they do to you is simply a mechanism that keeps them safe.

One size does not fit all when it comes to disciplinary consequences. Traditional punitive measures may not work for students who seem to disregard them. Instead, consider individualized approaches that address the specific needs and challenges of each student. Offer support and encouragement rather than focusing on punishment.

While some students may not care about consequences, they still benefit from clear expectations and boundaries. Communicate these rules effectively and consistently, emphasizing the importance of a respectful and positive learning environment for everyone. Be transparent about the consequences of not meeting expectations, even if the student appears indifferent.

Restorative practices are effective in resolving conflicts and building positive relationships between students and teachers. Instead of traditional punishments, focus on repairing harm and restoring the community when disciplinary issues arise. Engage the student in a reflective dialogue about their behavior and its impact on others.

Collaborate with school counselors, social workers, and administrators to create a network of support for the student. Engage in regular meetings to discuss strategies, progress, and additional resources that can assist the student in overcoming challenges.

Sometimes, students who don't care about consequences struggle academically, leading to disengagement. Offer additional academic support through tutoring, differentiated instruction, or individualized learning plans to help the student catch up and feel more competent in the classroom.

Help the student discover their intrinsic motivations for learning and personal growth. Encourage them to set goals, celebrate their progress, and take pride in their achievements. Cultivating intrinsic motivation can be a powerful tool in overcoming indifference towards consequences.

Maintain Boundaries

Dealing with challenging disciplinary situations can be emotionally draining. It is crucial to set boundaries and take care of your well-being. Seek support from colleagues, engage in self-care practices, and know when to involve school leadership if necessary.

It is essential to prioritize safety and maintain appropriate boundaries as an educator. Even if your intentions are pure, it is wise to never be alone with students to avoid any potential misunderstandings or misreporting in the future. Implement measures that provide clear safeguards and avoid any situation that could be questioned. When meeting with students, consider having another trusted adult present, someone whom the students know, like, and trust. By adopting these precautions, you ensure a professional and secure atmosphere that fosters trust and open communication.

Handling the most difficult disciplinary situations with students who don't seem to care about consequences requires patience, understanding, and adaptability. By fostering a safe and supportive environment, individualizing consequences and support, and seeking the involvement of supportive adults, teachers can make a significant impact on these students' lives. Remember that building positive relationships and cultivating intrinsic motivation are key components in helping students overcome indifference and reengage in the learning process.

Chapter 23: How to Celebrate Student Success

"People will work for money. But they will die for medals."

~ Winston Churchill

American businesswoman and author, Mary Kay Ash once quipped, "There are two things people want more than money: recognition and praise." Various surveys and studies have shown that employee recognition and appreciation are highly valued by workers in the United States and other countries. Many employees have expressed that feeling valued and appreciated for their work is a key contributor to their job satisfaction and motivation.

In some surveys, a significant number of American workers have indicated that they would prefer to receive recognition and appreciation for their efforts over a pay raise! (I'm not sure how many of those surveyed were teachers).

That said, trying to figure out what a child might want as a reward can be difficult. I hope in this chapter to give you effective ways to recognize student success and talk about how to reward students in a way that actually works.

We've covered setting goals and managing the classroom, and soon, your students are going to start achieving these goals, and behaving better. The way to get them continuously invested in setting goals and behaving well is to reward them. Of course, that's also the second "R" in the SMARTER goals framework.

1. Find Out What They Want

When it comes to rewarding students, one crucial step is to determine a specific reward and establish a clear deadline. This process can be particularly challenging in middle school, but it applies to all grade levels, be it elementary or high school. Take the time to decide on the reward that will motivate your students and set a deadline for when they can earn it.

Additionally, don't underestimate the power of asking your students for input. You might be surprised at how practical and feasible their suggestions can be. Engaging them in the process empowers them and makes the reward system more meaningful to their interests and preferences.

A pro tip: Don't be hesitant to explore paid options. There are funding resources available for such initiatives, so don't assume that you can't afford to offer certain rewards. Check with relevant decision-makers and inquire if there are funds allocated for student rewards. For instance, you might consider bringing in a Game Truck, which may initially seem out of budget, but you won't know until you ask. The worst outcome is a "no," but you might be pleasantly surprised by the support available.

In no particular order, here are 51 rewards ideas to get you started. They are a mixture of free and paid rewards.

Water Balloon Fight

Kickball Tournament

Teacher vs. Student Dodgeball

Extra Recess

Class Vs. Class Basketball Game

Movie Premier with Popcorn

Beanboozled Challenge

"Birthday" Party

Charades Competition

Pictionary Competition

Choose Teacher's Hairstyle

Teach Teacher a Dance

Choose Your Seat

Classwork Outside

Cotton Candy Party

Create a Class Handshake

Create a Class GIF

Create a Class MEME

Decorate a Ceiling Tile

Donate Party

Dress Down Day

Dress Up Day

Early Release to Lunch

Class Shoutout on School Website

Free Time

Freestyle Lunch ("Clubify" the Cafe)

Game Time

Graffiti Wall Decoration

Glow Party

Ice Cream Party

Use Teacher's First Name for a Day

K-9 Demonstration by Law Enforcement

Shoutout on Announcements

Lunch with Administrator

Minute to Win-it Games During Recess

Move Seats

Chill/Nap Time

Opposite Day

Headphones in Class

Pet Therapy Visit

Petting Zoo

Pie the Teacher

Pizza Party

Class Talent Show

Social Media Shoutout

Spirit Week

Sunglasses Day

Lip Sync Battle (Music or TikTok)

Selfie Station

Free Entry to a School Event

Dedicated Class Page in the Yearbook

Remember, there are plenty of free options for rewarding students, but be open to exploring paid options as well. What matters most is recognizing and celebrating the efforts and achievements of your students to foster a positive and motivated learning environment.

2. Get Them Excited!

Generate enthusiasm for the reward. Regardless of the specific reward, aim to ignite excitement among your students. While not everyone may share the same preferences, focus on building anticipation for the reward. It's akin to the anticipation leading up to New Year's celebrations, where everyone gets excited and counts down. Similarly, create that sense of anticipation for the reward, so your students are genuinely thrilled about the prospect of achieving it. By fostering excitement, you can fuel their motivation and engagement, making the reward even more rewarding for them.

3. Constant Reminders

Keep the reward at the forefront. Consistently bring up the reward students are striving for, especially before commencing the lesson. As a teacher, I used to display our goal and the corresponding reward on a slide right before starting the lesson. This practice served as a gentle reminder, ensuring students were always aware of what they were working towards. You might question whether this approach promotes intrinsic motivation, and I understand that concern. While it does involve external motivation, sometimes an external reward can help bolster intrinsic motivation. By consistently mentioning the reward, you reinforce the connection between effort and achievement, motivating students to stay focused and driven throughout the learning process.

4. Keep Your Word.

Honor your commitments. This is of utmost importance. Once you have set the reward and deadline, stick to them without wavering. Changing the reward or deadline can damage the trust you've built with your students. Consistency is key in maintaining a positive teacher-student relationship. Ensure that the chosen reward is realistic, achievable, and authorized, as once you commit, you must follow through. If you promise a reward, it is crucial to deliver it as promised. Failing to do so can make it difficult to regain the students' trust.

Let me share an example from my personal experience. My wife, Shakira, and I were babysitting our three-year-old niece. Whenever my wife called her over, the child wouldn't come. But as soon as Shakira said, "Come here, I have candy!" Our niece would come running. However, my wife didn't actually have any candy to offer. The next few times my wife called her with the promise of candy, our niece came running, but soon realized there was no candy and stopped responding to the false promise. Eventually when she was called to come over, she ignored us completely. Similarly, as teachers, offering rewards like pizza parties, pep rallies, or ice cream socials and then failing to deliver on them will erode students' trust, and they may start to resent the false promises.

To avoid this, make sure you commit to rewards and deadlines that you can fulfill. Show your students that you are dependable and that their efforts will be recognized and rewarded appropriately. This will not only keep them motivated but also strengthen your relationship with them, fostering a positive and conducive learning environment.

5. Be Sure to Reflect.

Reflect and celebrate. Reflection is a crucial part of the reward process, whether the students achieve the reward or not. Before they receive the reward, take a moment to reflect on their efforts and progress. For example, if you're heading to a pep rally, gather your students and say, "Today, we're heading to this pep rally because we achieved 75% content mastery on our earth science standards. You all did an amazing job, and we're incredibly proud of your hard work. Keep pushing yourselves, set higher goals, and continue to grow. You deserve this celebration, so go and have a fantastic time at the pep rally!"

Even if they don't earn the reward, it's essential to reflect. You can address the situation like this, "Today, we were supposed to have our pep rally because our goal was to reach 75% mastery. Unfortunately, we are currently at 62%, but that's okay. Our current condition is not our conclusion. We are not at 75% yet, but we can get there! We won't have the pep rally today, but we're going to stay in the classroom and keep working at it. We won't give up, and I know that with determination and perseverance, we will reach that 75% we're aiming for."

The key is to celebrate their progress and achievements, whether big or small. Acknowledge their hard work, determination, and growth, even if the ultimate goal is not met. Use reflection as a tool to motivate and encourage them to keep striving for success. By doing so, you foster a positive and supportive learning environment that empowers students to reach their full potential.

These are the strategies I use to effectively reward students. Whether it's an entire school, a grade level, a classroom, or an individual student, this framework can be adapted to suit various situations. Remember, it's crucial to develop student rewards that are practical, motivating, and aligned with your students' needs and preferences.

For digital resources such as templates to deliver a powerful reflection speech, visit:

www.onepercentamazing.com/resources

Bonus Section

Is School Leadership Right for You?

Chapter 24 – Life on the Other Side

"The tests we face in life's journey don't just reveal our weaknesses but help us discover our inner strengths. We can only know how strong we are when we strive and thrive beyond the challenges we face."

— Kemi Sogunle

I absolutely loved being a teacher, and I must admit, after I got the hang of it, I was pretty good at it. As you start to apply principles you learned in this book, and continue to improve as an educator, you will quickly learn how upward mobility works in education. When you become really skilled at your craft, the impact you have on your students is undeniable, and doors start opening to other opportunities.

That is why I included this bonus chapter. I already know that you are going to do so well that your impact won't be ignored, and soon doors will start opening. But I don't want you to just walk through doors because they open. I want you to carefully consider where the door leads, and if that's where you want to go. Many people view the ascension to school leadership as the appropriate trajectory for effective educators. But just like skinny jeans, school leadership is not for everybody. I want you to be as informed as possible when that door opens for you. I wasn't.

Without even petitioning for it, an opportunity was presented for me to step out of the classroom and into instructional coaching. I was on the fence for a while because I truly love teaching and leading a class of students. I was convinced when a mentor helped me to realize that by working directly with students, I alone could impact hundreds, but by empowering teachers we could affect millions. I was sold.

After instructional coaching for two years, and being a school administrator in the years since, as I reflect, I ask myself, "Was it the right decision for me?" Yes, I believe it was. However, it wasn't always crystal clear. Just like the start of my teaching career, the start of my school leadership career was rocky. The fact that I stepped into school leadership right as the world shut down in 2019 might've had a teeny bit to do with that, but nonetheless, I struggled. I quickly realized that the new path I chose wasn't exactly what I had envisioned. It had its challenges and wasn't everything I thought it would be. I made my fair share of mistakes along the way. Yet, those mistakes became valuable lessons that contributed to my growth as an educator.

So, I will close this book by sharing with you the five essential school leadership lessons I've learned that will help you get a clear picture of life on the other side. You will also be given a checklist to help decide if school leadership is the next step for you.

Honorable Mention

First and foremost, as a school leader, you'll find that the majority of your interactions will be with adults rather than students. Initially, I thought that being an instructional leader would allow me the flexibility to engage with students directly, coaching and mentoring them. However, as I stepped into the leadership role, I realized that those interactions with students wouldn't occur naturally; I had to be proactive about making time for them. It's easy to get caught up in paperwork, data analysis, discipline referrals, meetings, observations, parent concerns, busing logistics, building maintenance, club/activity organization, testing administration, community engagement, and all the other things school leaders do. It makes it very hard to have those meaningful interactions with students in the classrooms, on the field, or in affinity groups. While observations and checking on teachers are essential aspects of your role, connecting with students on a personal level requires intentional effort; otherwise, you risk losing that vital aspect of being an educator.

During my time as a school administrator, I quickly realized that if I wanted to maintain meaningful relationships with students, I had to go the extra mile. This meant being present on the bus lot, making time in my schedule to engage with students during car line pickups, and intentionally seeking opportunities to interact with them throughout the day.

If you're someone who doesn't mind primarily dealing with adults and is seeking a role with less student interaction, then this path may be suitable for you. However, if you're like me, and you thrive on the joy of connecting with students, I would caution against leaving the classroom too soon. As a teacher, you have the unique opportunity to immerse yourself in students' lives daily, impacting their education and personal growth. Becoming an administrator may distance you from that direct connection with students, so carefully consider your passion for student interaction before making the transition. There are undoubtedly valuable experiences and challenges that come with being an administrator, but it's essential to assess whether the trade-off is right for you and if it aligns with your career goals and aspirations.

Lesson Number 5

It is not easy to replicate yourself. As a matter of fact, it is impossible (depending on when you are reading this book. I heard scientists are getting close). The reason why I say that is because, being an awesome teacher doesn't mean you can make awesome teachers. I like to use the example of hiring Taylor Swift as a vocal coach. Taylor Swift is an amazing singer, performer, entertainer, and overall person. She is able to do things that others only dream of doing. She has worked to create a legacy that will last a lot longer than she will, but if you hire her to be your vocal coach, you won't become Taylor Swift. You might improve. You may gain some skills, but you most likely won't be able to replicate her success. This principle is the same in schools.

You being an awesome teacher has a tremendous impact on your students, but just because you have found strategies to help your students have tremendous success does not mean that you will be able to coach someone else to do the same. We talked about it a lot in this book; your unique differences allow you to make your unique impact. Before you decide to move on, carefully consider what you are leaving behind.

Working as a school leader has taught me a valuable lesson: not every teacher shares the same level of dedication and passion for their role. Initially, I believed that all struggling teachers simply needed more coaching and support to improve their skills. I saw myself as the coach who could help them excel in their profession.

However, I soon realized that the issue isn't always about lacking skills; it's sometimes a matter of lacking the will to do what is necessary. There are teachers who show up just for the paycheck, without a genuine desire to do what's best for the students. I know this, because I have been explicitly told this by a (former) teacher that I was coaching. No strategy, resource, or coaching model can fix that.

And for the teachers that have the will, their zone of excellence is different than yours. So, the impact that they make, even if it's effective, may come through a different approach. For this reason, a great coach understands that the goal is not to make the next best version of you, but the very best version of themselves. A great coach will support them through the journey of learning how to leverage their uniqueness to drive educational transformation, which is not easy.

If you're someone who can certifiably bring out the best in others, helping them to maximize their potential to have a massive impact, and are ready to turn over the keys to your classroom, then a leadership position might be suitable for you.

On the other hand, if you are amazing at what you do, and are having a tremendous impact on the lives of students, you may already be living in your purpose. Taylor Swift doesn't need to coach singers right now; she needs to keep singing. Some amazing teachers don't need to coach teachers right now, they need to keep teaching. If the thought of giving up teaching causes you pause, then school leadership might not be the right fit for you at this time.

Lesson Number 4

It's difficult for me to admit, but I keep hearing the same phrase repeatedly from my mentors and the people I talk to, and I have found it to be true for me as well: "It's lonely at the top." My situation involved a promotion within the same school where I had friends and close relationships. I had hoped that despite the change in my title and position, I could maintain those connections. However, I quickly realized that when my title switched, my friends did too.

Numerous times, I have walked into a room and noticed that people straighten up or stop talking. This doesn't happen with everyone, but quite a few people. I distinctly remember during my first year in school leadership I had an awkward situation with four teachers I used to share laughs and jokes with. I strolled into the classroom like I was accustomed to doing, but this time the atmosphere became tense, and they quickly change the topic as if they were planning a surprise party that they didn't want me to hear about. Since that was four years ago and I have yet to experience a surprise party, I assume that they were discussing something they didn't want me to overhear, perhaps even talking about me. It was clear they no longer saw me as a friend but as a member of the leadership team they needed to be cautious around.

What stands out to me the most is that I haven't changed as a person; I'm still the same understanding and nonjudgmental individual I was before. Yet, it seems that some people became uncomfortable around me when I was given a position of authority. I sought advice from my principal, the dean, and a mentor who is a principal, and they all used the same phrase: "It's lonely at the top." They too experienced people treating them differently because of their status and title, regardless of their unchanged character.

The clearest example of this dynamic that I can give occurred at our staff outing a few years ago while I was still teaching. It was a Winter celebration just for staff and most of us were there. We rented a section at a popular spot near the school, and paid for everyone's food and fountain drinks, but alcohol had to be purchased separately. The event was from 6pm-10pm the night before Winter Break. Everybody was hanging out, playing games, and talking. I remember that I was talking to my principal right around 8pm, and she said, "Well, let me get out of here so everyone can have some fun." I was confused and asked her what she meant. She said, "They won't loosen up if I'm in here, so for events like this, I come to show my face, and I leave so they can enjoy themselves." That stuck with me. As the social butterfly that I am, I don't want to have to leave a party so that people can have fun.

I will remind you that these tips are based on my experience. Perhaps you know of or are an administrator that has very close personal relationships with everyone you supervise. That hasn't been my experience.

If your school is where you have the majority of your friendships, moving into a leadership role might cause your social circle to shrink. If you do not primarily rely on your school environment to build your core group of friends, then taking on a leadership position might not affect your social circle too much.

Lesson Number 3

When I transitioned into a school leadership role, I anticipated a constant barrage of tasks, from meetings and observations to scheduling and data analysis. While there is indeed a lot to accomplish, I discovered that I have more control over when these tasks are completed, as long as they are met by the designated deadline.

As a teacher, my days followed a set schedule, with specific times for classes, lunch, and recess. However, in school leadership, the focus shifts more towards accomplishing tasks within the given deadlines. For the most part, I have the freedom to design my own schedule to ensure all responsibilities are fulfilled on time. But just because my schedule is flexible, doesn't mean it is lighter. The deadlines carry a lot more weight.

It is crucial to recognize that missing deadlines in a school leadership position can have severe consequences. Take school-wide testing preparation for example. From scheduling, to making sure accommodations are given, to Chromebook cart allocation, and all other things related to local testing, it is important to make sure it is done efficiently. In my case, it is a team effort, and a few amazing people work with me on this, but that doesn't take much pressure off. If I were to miss a single deadline, there would be significant disruptions to the testing schedule, impacting students, parents, and staff alike. A teacher missing deadlines often has to deal with students and a few parents. An administrator who misses deadlines often has to deal with the whole school community. No pressure.

If you are someone who can create your own schedule and prioritize tasks based on given deadlines, this role will likely suit you well. On the other hand, if you rely heavily on a strict schedule to stay on track with your work, this position may not be the best fit for you. It requires a level of adaptability and responsibility to manage tasks effectively within their designated timeframes. It's a delicate balance that must be struck... a dance, if you will.

Lesson Number 2

One of the most significant lessons I've learned as an administrator is that it's impossible to please everyone. No matter how thoughtful, well-intentioned, and well-informed your decisions are, there will always be individuals who disagree or have different perspectives. This is a fundamental truth of life, and it becomes even more pronounced in a leadership position where the spotlight is on you and various stakeholders have diverse expectations.

To complicate things even further, while you want to be a supportive figure for everyone, not everyone will resonate with every approach. I've always chosen to maintain a positive mindset and wear a smile on my face, finding the silver linings even in challenging situations. However, I've encountered feedback from some individuals who interpret this as gaslighting or toxic positivity. It's disheartening to hear, but I had to recognize that people perceive and respond to things differently.

The truth is, not everyone will appreciate or connect with my demeanor, and that's completely fine. Each person has their preferences and ways of processing situations. Some may find my positivity inspiring and uplifting, while others may view it as irritating or insincere. Understanding this has helped me accept that I am not everyone's cup of tea. Being honest, neither are you.

Early on I tried to be the leader that everyone was looking for, rather than the leader I was called to be. Now, instead of trying to please everyone, my focus is on being the best version of myself that I can be. I've chosen to deliberately show up each day with authenticity, compassion, and a positive outlook. As long as I stay true to myself and my values, I know that I'm doing my best.

Recognizing that I can't be everything for everybody has been a humbling experience. It has taught me the importance of staying true to myself while respecting others' perspectives. By being genuine and consistent in my actions, I can continue to inspire those who connect with my approach, and still support those that may not. It is a challenging balancing act, but it is possible.

And it doesn't just stop with the teachers who you support. Each decision that is made has far-reaching consequences, and not everyone will be satisfied with the outcome. Some students, teachers, families, board members, or district representatives may express dissatisfaction, and it's crucial to acknowledge that this is part of the role.

The key takeaway from this experience is the necessity of developing tough skin and having confidence in your decision-making process. As an administrator, I've had to learn how to be unwavering in my commitment to making choices that are in the best interest of the school community as a whole. It's about weighing the available information, considering various perspectives, and ultimately arriving at the decision that aligns with the vision for the school's success.

If you are thinking about school leadership, remember that leadership often demands making tough choices. You will have to embrace the fact that you won't always be popular, but that can't be your primary goal. Your focus should be on creating an environment that fosters student success, teacher growth, and a positive school culture.

Every decision we make, every new initiative we roll out, comes with the possibility of either success or failure. But promise me something, whether you win or lose, be sure that you learn. Life is full of wins and losses, but most importantly, it is an endless journey of learning and growth.

If you aren't ready to embrace the vulnerability that comes with making decisions in a public space, admit to missteps, and be hated by those whom you want to be loved by, then pursuing a school leadership position may not be the right move at this time. It takes a willingness to grow and learn, coupled with the ability to withstand criticism and opposition, to thrive in a leadership role. If you are mentally strong enough to withstand scrutiny, defend your decisions, and remain authentic no matter what, then you might be ready to move into a leadership position.

Lesson Number 1

Most importantly, I need you to remember that, despite having a higher salary and more responsibilities, school leaders are still as human as anyone else in the building. (Don't perceive the increased salary as a subtle boast, it's just a well-known fact; school leaders are paid more than teachers.) However, having a higher salary and greater responsibilities doesn't diminish a person's humanity. School leaders have emotions, feelings, and vulnerabilities just like everyone else. I still experience the same range of emotions as I did as a teacher. I get hurt, burnt out, tired, and stressed at times. As an administrator, I often find myself working tirelessly to ensure that everyone else has what they need, but in the process, I sometimes neglect taking care of myself. It's easy to feel overwhelmed and forget the importance of self-care.

If you're considering moving into administration, I want this to be a crucial message for you: remember that you're still human. Despite the added responsibilities and demands, you must prioritize your well-being. Taking time for yourself, practicing self-care, and setting boundaries are vital aspects of maintaining your effectiveness and mental health as an administrator.

Don't lose sight of the fact that you need to recharge and take care of your own needs in order to effectively support others. It's not selfish; it's a necessity. Recognizing your limits and taking time for self-care is crucial to preventing burnout and ensuring that you can continue to make a positive impact as a school leader. The message from Chapter 4 still holds true; your best ability is your availability. Nothing else matters if you are unavailable to show up.

Striking a balance between fulfilling your responsibilities and caring for yourself will not only benefit you, but also empower you to better serve the school community. Remember, you're still human, and taking care of yourself is essential for your overall well-being and success as an administrator.

As promised, here is a checklist to help you decide if making the move from teaching to school leadership is right for you. If you answer "yes" to 8 out of 10 questions, you just might be ready for school leadership. For a digital version of this checklist, visit:

www.onepercentamazing.com/resources

So, You Want To Be An Administrator...

1. Do you want to spend most of your time with adults?

2. Can you handle being ignored?

3. Do you do well with prioritizing tasks?

4. Are you strong enough to be hated?

5. Are you comfortable making mistakes in public?

6. Can you anticipate problems be proactive instead of reactive?

7. Do you connect with the culture of the school?

8. Will you be fine socially if your coworkers are not your friends?

9.If your efforts are not appreciated, can you keep showing up?

10. Do you have a strong self-care routine?

Conclusion

If you view your 1% as a deficiency, you'll operate as if it is. If you view your 1% as your "amazing," you'll operate with confidence.

The process of learning to leverage your uniqueness will show the elements that have the power to make you an effective teacher, and have the most impact on the students looking to you for knowledge. No longer will you need to hide what makes you different; from this day on, you will highlight it!

Whether you are a teacher, an administrator, a school board member or a parent, you can support this global movement to transform our schools by helping each individual classroom reach its goals.

The status quo is no longer sufficient. Consistently showing up to teach in places that don't celebrate your individuality and unique approach is not sustainable. You deserve more. Your mental health, your family's financial security, and your students demand better. By increasing your efficacy, you can make a lasting difference in the lives of the human beings in your class. It is time to live your dream, illuminate your uniqueness, and change the world one class at a time. Indeed, it is time to be the transformative teacher you were always meant to be.

For teachers who truly want to be teachers, I want you to finally believe that you have what it takes. All you need is that 1% that takes you from ordinary to extraordinary and goals that will help you unleash the best in yourself, your colleagues, and your students.

The work of education is hard. This is true. For those of us who understand what is at stake, we don't mind the grind. We signed up for this! We want to teach because we know that teachers can impact the world through education in the most positive way. We just need to know how to do it effectively. With all the roadblocks removed, we can truly shine.

If you've been jaded by the system and feel like Sisyphus in Greek mythology endless pushing the rock up the hill only to see it roll down again, you now have the answer to the biggest question teachers have been asking. You have the blueprint for success. Your job is simply to implement it.

Now that you have clarity in your purpose and efficacy in your practice, nothing can stop you. I bid you the greatest of success. You've got this, and I've got you.

"The influence of teachers extends beyond the classroom, touching eternity through the seeds

of knowledge and wisdom they plant in the
hearts and minds of their students." - Plato

About the Author

Daryl Williams Jr. is a man of excellence and a shining example of how excellence, when pursued, can be achieved. His career in education has seen him teach, coach, and now administer to those under his watch. His talents go far beyond this as his larger-than-life persona is infectious to anyone with whom he interacts; motivating them both inside and outside the classroom to achieve excellence. Known not only for his resonating words but also his enthralling energy, Daryl's style gives his talks an enduring impact no matter the size or event.

He started by teaching middle school math for six years before taking the step forward to become an Instructional Coach. His hard work resulted in him garnering a National Board Certification, two Teacher of the Year awards, and not one - but two - Master's Degrees from Johns Hopkins University and The University of North Carolina, respectively. Currently in the role of Assistant Principal, he continues to make strides as he works to support educators in elevating their classroom practices to enhance student growth.

Through his company, Pursuit of Excellence, Daryl has made it his mission to help a million students live the life they have chosen rather than the life they are forced to settle for. He works hard to create resources that develop important skills, mindset, and character strengths in students as well as leading professional development sessions and producing online content to encourage teachers and school leaders on how best to nurture their students' growth. It is clear that Daryl cares deeply about each and every student he strives to help and his work in education is only beginning.

HAVE DARYL WILLIAMS JR. EMPOWER YOUR STUDENTS, TEACHERS, OR DISTRICT!

Daryl Williams Jr. offers programs to impact every level of learner. His "Choices" Program features student assemblies and curriculum designed to help students build skills now, so that they have choices later. He leads staff professional development to extend the strategies mentioned in this book, as well as other cutting age student growth strategies. His 99% A Human, 1% Amazing keynote is sought after by districts across the nation that are looking to empower educators to overcome stress, avoid burnout, and create impactful change. Scan the code below or visit www.darylwilliamsjr.com for booking information.

Let's Connect!

@DARYLWILLIAMS_ _

WHAT ARE PEOPLE SAYING ABOUT DARYL WILLIAMS JR.'S PROGRAMS?

Students

"Sometimes I think I can't do this…but with his "Y.E.T" speech, I think to myself, I can't do this, yet."

"It's really important that everyone gets to know this. You may not be able to do it right now, but you can do it eventually."

"I feel a lot more empowered, and a lot more confident..I have been really stressed out about college, [thinking] I can't do it, and stuff like that. But now I feel like I can do it if I really work towards it."

Teachers

"The message was inspiring and relevant for newer and/or younger educators, and can serve as a refreshing reminder for veterans that may be burning out or becoming a bit apathetic. It helps to refocus and reevaluate on the why as well as the what of what we do as well as serve to inspire us to connect with our students in a way that only we can; this ultimately leads to greater success."

"It was very enlightening. I had so much that I realized about myself as a person and what I can be as a teacher. It was one of the most amazing speeches to listen to. I loved it!"

"He was real, and I loved being surrounded by someone who was truly passionate about impacting education from the top down!!"

"Very informative and inspirational. Sparks motivation to help students but also to keep your passion for learning."

"Motivating! Reminded me of why I am an educator and continue to get up everyday and do my job."

Made in the USA
Monee, IL
01 February 2024

52662234R00164